Management Wisdom in Thirukkural

R. Mananathan

INDIA • SINGAPORE • MALAYSIA

Copyright © R. Mananathan 2025
All Rights Reserved.

ISBN

Paperback 979-8-89699-920-1
Hardcase 979-8-89777-631-3

This book has been published with all efforts taken to make the material error-free after the consent of the author. However, the author and the publisher do not assume and hereby disclaim any liability to any party for any loss, damage, or disruption caused by errors or omissions, whether such errors or omissions result from negligence, accident, or any other cause.

While every effort has been made to avoid any mistake or omission, this publication is being sold on the condition and understanding that neither the author nor the publishers or printers would be liable in any manner to any person by reason of any mistake or omission in this publication or for any action taken or omitted to be taken or advice rendered or accepted on the basis of this work. For any defect in printing or binding the publishers will be liable only to replace the defective copy by another copy of this work then available.

Dedicated to my loving mother

Navaneedham Ammal

who carved me into what I am today

Contents

Preface

In the history of humanity, many scholars and saints have been born in different parts of the world and have preached discipline to the society to make the people live in peace and harmony. Prophets like Jesus, Mohammed, and Buddha preached religious paths to show the right way of living. Scholars like Socrates, Confucius and Aristotle enlightened the masses with rational thinking. All these saints and scholars were preaching discipline mostly embracing their religion and culture prevailing wherever they lived.

But, one scholar, a poet and a genius, namely Thiruvalluvar from Tamil Nadu, India was different. He wrote a book by the name Thirukkural to preach discipline, honesty and a virtuous way of living. His teachings were beyond any religion, race, language or country. They were universal and generic, pertinent to humanity in total. Thiruvalluvar, shortly called Valluvar, has not mentioned the name of any religion in his book, though, there were many religions practiced during his period. This literary work was written in THAMIZH language, which, in recent times is being pronounced as TAMIL. Thiruvalluvar was born around the third century BC in the Chola Kingdom of Tamil Nadu, which is situated in the southernmost part of today's India.

Tamil is an ancient language spoken by Tamilians (Tamils). Seventy five million Tamils are living in Tamil Nadu and another 15 million people living in other countries like Sri Lanka, Malaysia, Singapore, United States etc. Tamil is probably the only language in which maximum number (many thousands) of literary works have been written. These literary works cover multifarious subjects like art, culture, love, music, heroism, spirituality, philosophy, religion etc. All these works were written during the pre-printing era in seasoned palm leaves.

Thirukkural was written on palm leaves as well. Thirukkural contains 1330 couplets (short poems). Each couplet is only two sentences long, consisting of four words in the first line and three words in the second line. Valluvar has maintained this structure in all the 1330 couplets.

Thirukkural contains three major **PARTS** called Paal (பால்) in Tamil. These three PARTS are subdivided into **CHAPTERS** called 'Athigaram' (அதிகாரம்) in Tamil. There are 133 chapters and each chapter consists of ten **COUPLETS** called kural (குறள்) in Tamil, totaling 1330 couplets.

PART-1:   **VIRTUE - 38 Chapters - 380 Couplets**
                           (Teaches Virtuous Life)

PART-2:   **WEALTH - 70 Chapters - 700 Couplets**
                           (Teaches Materialistic Life)

PART-3:   **LOVE - 25 Chapters - 250 Couplets**
                           (Teaches Fair Love)

Every chapter is given an appropriate heading relevant to the subject it handles. In the 1330 couplets, Valluvar has narrated a practical way of living with good virtues, making wealth and living with pleasure. We can say, Thirukkural is an encyclopedia of Life Science. It analyses every bit of human life and teaches the best way of living and co-living. Thirukkural does not teach spirituality, though in the first chapter namely "Hail the GOD" Valluvar has written ten couplets emphasizing the importance of worshipping GOD who is the creator of the world. Valluvar has mentioned only GOD in his book and did not attribute the GOD to any religion. Rest, he talks of various life science subjects such as discipline, education, friendship, economy, social justice, advice to rulers, managing the kingdom, making wealth etc. In the third part LOVE he talks of premarital love between two sexes. A poet teaching a disciplined way of life, allotting a PART for LOVE is something very rare and unique. He has written this chapter, probably because he has understood that procreation is the ultimate goal of GOD to maintain the **Perpetual Cycle** created by him. Discussing more on the Perpetual Cycle is beyond the scope of this book.

Though Thirukkural preaches various life science subjects, I am focusing only on those couplets that are relevant to today's Modern Management Practices. I have selected seventy two couplets which teach a high level of management philosophy. I have also added a few more couplets in between to support these couplets.

Some of you may ask a question: "How could a poet who lived two thousand years back write about Modern Management Principles?"

The King and the GOD

Every human being prays to GOD to get rid of his problems and to get what he desires. But, in most cases the result is subjective. It is a kind of 'Yes or No' by GOD. Human beings have become accustomed to accept both.

But, if a king wants, he can solve most of the problems faced by his citizens and meet most of their desires. In other words, the king is a God for his citizens. Even today, in many countries, the people of the country treat their rulers as GOD. Such being the case, it becomes very important for the king to be a 'Good King'. Otherwise, it will be a disaster for the country and its citizens. Probably for this reason, most of the scholars and saints who lived on those days advised the kings on good governance. Some scholars went to the extent of fighting with the king demanding fair governance. Valluvar too in his book Thirukkural, has given many advices to the king on good governance.

Advice to the King and Modern Management Principles

These advices, given by him to a king, are very relevant for today's business leaders also. Just by replacing the following words in the couplets with the words given, the meanings of the couplets become the best Management Principles being followed today.

King:	**Managing Director or CEO**
Minister:	**Manager**
Country:	**Organisation or company**
Enemy:	**Competitor**
Envoy:	**Marketing Manager**
Espionage:	**Market Intelligence**

This means that, the philosophy of management is the same whether for a king or an entrepreneur. Principles are principles and do not differ between an empire and a business.

There are books already written by many Tamil scholars and professors on 'Management by Valluvar'. But, this book carries my fifty years of management experience to support the points put forth by Valluvar and their synonymity for today's business.

Any entrepreneur reading this book will learn to take all precautions in business, commit fewer mistakes and take the right decisions. Wherever relevant I have shared my personal experience in Business Management. I have also quoted the experience of many successful entrepreneurs whose success can be traced back to Valluvar's teachings. I have taken much care in not altering the couplet's meaning as depicted by Valluvar and I have also taken care to ensure the English translation does not alter the meaning as well.

To make the reading cheerful I have brought two characters in the book, a son and a father, wherein the son asks questions and the father answers him to explain the couplets and the management aspects in it.

I express my thanks to Prof. S. Arumugam, Vice Chancellor of Tamilnadu Open University for offering an excellent Foreword for this book.

R.Mananathan   Puducherry
Chairman, Manatec Group of Companies   14-01-2025
Puducherry, India.
mananathan@manatec.in

Foreword

It is with great pleasure that I write this foreword for the book, **"Management Wisdom in Thirukkural"** by R. Mananathan. This work masterfully explores how the timeless wisdom of Thiruvalluvar, as encapsulated in *Thirukkural*, aligns seamlessly with contemporary management practices. By bridging ancient philosophy with modern-day applications in human resources, marketing, research and development, project management, and much more, this book serves as a testament to the enduring relevance of Valluvar's teachings.

Thirukkural is universally regarded as a treasure trove of ethical, social, and philosophical insights. What makes it extraordinary is its ability to transcend time and offer solutions to modern challenges. In this book, the author highlights the practical wisdom embedded in *Thirukkural* and how it can guide individuals and organizations in making informed, ethical, and visionary decisions.

Through engaging narratives and detailed analysis, the book presents Valluvar's couplets in a format that resonates with today's readers. The coupling of timeless wisdom with concepts like SWOT analysis, PERT charts, FMEA methodologies, and strategies for motivation and communication demonstrates the author's deep understanding of both management principles and classical Tamil literature.

This book also addresses the critical facets of business initiation, planning, and execution, offering insights drawn from *Thirukkural* that emphasize thorough preparation, clarity in decision-making, and the significance of time and resource management. The lessons articulated here are invaluable for aspiring entrepreneurs, seasoned managers, and students of management alike.

The author's unique approach to interpreting *Thirukkural* for today's dynamic business environment is commendable. His ability to draw parallels between ancient couplets and contemporary management practices reaffirms the relevance of classical wisdom in shaping future strategies.

This book also stands out in its conversational style, where a father imparts knowledge to his son. This engaging format not only simplifies complex concepts but also serves as an excellent guide for readers of all ages. The practical examples provided—ranging from infrastructure projects like the Delhi Metro to the construction of the Burj Khalifa—offer invaluable insights into the application of Valluvar's principles in real-world scenarios.

As the Vice Chancellor of Tamil Nadu Open University, which is dedicated to empowering learners from all walks of life, I am particularly heartened by the emphasis this book places on ethical and well-thought-out decision-making in business. It serves as a reminder that success in any venture is rooted in values, clarity of purpose, and a commitment to excellence—qualities that Thiruvalluvar has immortalized through his couplets.

I congratulate R. Mananathan for this scholarly contribution and recommend this book to anyone interested in understanding the fusion of ancient knowledge with modern management concepts. It is an indispensable resource for those seeking ethical, inclusive, and sustainable approaches to management and leadership.

Let us take inspiration from Valluvar's insights, apply them in our professional lives, and strive to achieve excellence while upholding ethical principles.

Prof. S. Arumugam

12-01-2025

Vice Chancellor
Tamil Nadu Open University
Chennai-India

VALLUVAR'S ADVICE
TO
START A BUSINESS

1.0 Starting a Business

Son: Dad, how can Valluvar who lived in an era of a few hundred years BC, give ideas for starting a business today?

Father: That's a good question. First of all, you must know the knowledge of Thiruvalluvar. He has been an extraordinary person and might have been a genius. If you read all his couplets, you will appreciate the depth of knowledge he might have possessed in worldly affairs. Since he has written the couplets in a generic manner, they are apt for today's situations also. To prove his knowledge, I will give an example to you. In one of the couplets he says,

சுழன்றும் ஏர்ப்பின்னது உலகம் அதனால்
உழந்தும் உழவே தலை. (குறள் - 1031)

Though the earth is spinning, it is behind a plough only; therefore agriculture leads the world. (Couplet - 1031)

The idea is simple and understandable. Agriculture leads the world. But, the analogy given by him in this couplet, uses a word in Tamil '*சுழன்றும்*' meaning, the earth is rotating or spinning. In Valluvar's days, everyone was thinking that the earth was a **flat** object. Only in the year 1500 AD, during Galileo's period, it was scientifically proved that the earth is spinning. It is surprising to note that Valluvar knew two thousand years back that the earth was rotating. This proves that Valluvar had an extraordinary knowledge. If you read the book Thirukkural fully you will come across many such examples and you will accept that he should have been a genius. Valluvar was a great thinker too.

Valluvar, being a visionary who can imagine the future, has understood the fact that, business will also become imperative for human beings for their livelihood besides agriculture. For this reason, he has written many couplets, spread over many chapters, about carrying out business, apart from offering advice on virtues and values. It is a wonder that these suggestions remain highly relevant for today's modern management also.

Son, in today's situation, doing business is not an easy task. It requires versatile capabilities. Therefore, only those individuals, who have such special qualities, can indulge in business. For such of those who decide to do business, Valluvar gives many suggestions right from starting the business. Now, let us see some of his couplets which teach the precautions to be taken before starting a business.

1.1   Couplet: 467 / Chapter: 47
Knowledgeable Execution (தெரிந்து செயல் வகை)

எண்ணித் துணிக கருமம் துணிந்தபின்
எண்ணுவம் என்பது இழுக்கு.

Think before embarking on a job. It will be a blunder to think after embarking.

Son: Dad, this couplet is very simple and easy to understand. Is there anything special in this couplet?

Father: This couplet is applicable for performing any kind of job. Here 'job' means any activity or business. Valluvar has touched upon a very important point. He says that one must think well before acting. Many people act impulsively without applying the mind in advance and regret later for not considering certain factors. For such people, Valluvar advises them to be more vigilant before starting any venture.

Son: Dad, why hasn't Valluvar mentioned specific steps or methods for applying one's mind in advance?

Father: Yes. He hasn't. This is the characteristic of Valluvar's teachings. Anything he has said is **universal and generic and applicable** to every activity a person can accomplish. The methods may vary for different businesses though the principle is the same. Therefore he has not mentioned any specific steps or methods to apply the mind. By giving just a **hint** in two short sentences (exactly seven words), he expects the readers to apply their minds to elaborate on the hints given by him for any specific activity which they are undertaking. This method of **'hint and leave to think'** can be seen in all his couplets.

Son: Dad, I am interested in starting a manufacturing industry. What are the points to be thought of in advance?

Father: Well. To start a manufacturing industry, I am listing some important points to be planned in advance.

- The **product** to be manufactured.

- The **technology** for manufacturing the product.

- The **process** of manufacturing.

- The **machinery** required.

- A **market study** to know the market potential.

- The **competition** existing in the market.

- The ways of **tackling the competition.**

- The **investment** required.

- The **profit** expected.

- etc.

All these points have to be considered before embarking on a business mission. Lots of data have to be collected for each point and these data must be analysed and converted into a **Project Report**. This project report must be thorough and flawless and might require many revisions before finalizing. All the possible pitfalls must be anticipated in advance and remedies must be evolved beforehand. Valluvar has given a hint using a single word '*எண்ணி*' meaning **'think'**. When this word is elaborated, it results in a detailed document called the Project Report. If the preparation is for a war, the meaning of 'think' will be different.

Instead of planning in advance, if someone decides to start a business with the idea of making decisions as he progresses, then, what will happen? He will face unexpected challenges and problems. In today's management theory also, this point is insisted in the form of **Project Planning** before starting any industry or business. Particularly, big businesses are started only after preparing a **Detailed Project Report (DPR)**. Valluvar has written this couplet as applicable for all businesses or ventures at all times.

Son: Can you give some examples of 'well-planned' executions?

Father: Many successful projects can be cited as examples of this.

1. **Indira Gandhi International Airport in Delhi** was constructed in a record time of four years with ultra-modern facilities. This is because of the selection of the right technology, process, clear planning and teamwork.

2. **New Delhi Metro Phase I** was constructed in a short period of six years due to meticulous planning.

3. The world's tallest building **Burj Khalifa** in Dubai was constructed in a record time of six years. This is an example of well-planned execution.

Many more examples can be given.

Plan in advance to avoid regrets later!

1.2   Couplet: 675 / Chapter: 68
Mode of Execution (வினைசெயல்வகை)

பொருள்கருவி காலம் வினைஇடனொடு ஐந்தும்
இருள்தீர எண்ணிச் செயல்.

***Before venturing, get absolute clarity on these five;
the product, machinery, time, process and location.***

Son: Dad, I think Valluvar explains the important decisions to be taken while starting a business.

Father: Yes. You are right. Today's management experts also insist on taking clear decisions on the five points before venturing into any business.

1. The **Product** to be manufactured

2. The **Machinery** required

3. The **Time** for completion

4. The **Process** of manufacturing

5. The **Location** of business

According to Valluvar, the above points must be thoroughly evaluated and careful decisions have to be taken before starting a business. Valluvar uses a word in Tamil 'இருள்தீர' which means 'taking decisions with absolute clarity and without any doubt or grey area'. In other words, he means the decisions taken must be flawless.

Son: Yes Dad. I can appreciate this point. Now that I have decided to start a manufacturing industry, I have to decide on the product to be manufactured. Valluvar has not told how to select the product to be manufactured. Can you give me some ideas?

Father: I have already told you that Valluvar normally tells us **'what to do'** and leaves **'How to do'** to our decision. Let me explain how to select a product. To be frank, this is a million-dollar question and is tough to answer. Nevertheless, I will provide you with certain guidelines. In simple terms, **any product which has a market** can be chosen.

Son: How to find out whether the product has a market?

Father: You can conduct a **Market Survey** and assess the market potential for the product. You can employ specialists to carry out a market survey. Identify the competitors and their market share. Also, measure the annual **Market Growth** of the product which adds to the market potential. From these data, you can arrive at the **Market Gap**.

Market Gap = Market Potential + Market Growth - Competitor's Share

This Market Gap can be filled by you.

Son: If the Market Gap is minimum or NIL what to do?

Father: If there is no 'Market Gap' even after considering annual growth, it is better not to select this product, unless you have some special features or **Unique Selling Points (USPs)** in your product to capture a share from the competition. **Innovation** always provides an opportunity to capture a market share from the competition.

Son: Can 'price' be a factor, to decide the product?

Father: Certainly. If the quality and features are at par with the competition in the market and if you can sell your product at a lesser price, then go ahead and select the product even if the 'market gap' is NIL. All the above questions must arise on reading the term 'Product', in this couplet. If these questions do not arise to an individual, then he becomes unfit to start a business.

Son: Valluvar uses the word 'விளைவ' in Tamil which I understand as the Process. Am I right?

Father: Yes. You are right. The process of manufacturing determines the **Cost, Time and Quality (CTQ)** of a product. Today there are many different processes available for manufacturing a product like Fully Automatic, Semi-Automatic and Manual. There are 'high speed' and 'low speed' options as well. You must select a process which is well established, proven and complies with the CTQ parameters of the product chosen. If the product has to comply with certain technical standards like DIN, NEMA, ASTM, BIS, SAE, etc., then the process must accommodate the standard requirements. Selection of the process must be carefully done because it cannot be changed once selected.

Son: Dad, Valluvar has mentioned 'machinery' in this couplet. How to select the right machinery to produce the product?

Father: The process selected determines the machinery required. For manufacturing a product, many different machinery choices are available. Very expensive machinery manufactured by western countries are available in the market, as well as some affordable options from China. The decision must be taken based on the type of production, such as Batch Production or Mass Production. **Return on Investment** is another parameter to be considered to decide the right machinery.

Son: Having decided on the Product, Process and Machinery, Valluvar says the manufacturing facility must be at the right location. How to choose the right location?

Father: The location for a manufacturing industry has to be chosen based on many parameters like,

- Availability of raw materials and skilled manpower.

- Accessibility to the marketplace

- Availability of logistic facilities like Couriers, Trucks, Port facilities etc.

- Considering the Government concessions like subsidies, tax holidays etc.

- Special facilities like Export Processing Zones (EPZ), Special Economic Zones (SEZ) etc.

In deciding a location, the cost implications of the above parameters must be weighed one against the other and the final decision must be taken. Eventually, one must choose a location that will result in the least cost of production. This is a serious decision, because, once the project is implemented, the location cannot be changed.

My experience:

Son, I wish to share my experience on this subject. In 1987, I started to manufacture my first product called **Shaft Alignment Computer**. This product was my innovation developed out of my experience in alignment and vibration technologies. This is a high-tech product involving electronic Hardware and Software. I started this project in my native village namely 'Keezh kumara mangalam' in the interest of developing my village. But, only after starting the project, I did realize that manufacturing this product required highly qualified specialists having experience in high-tech hardware and software. Unfortunately, such qualified candidates were neither available in my village nor in the nearby city of Pondicherry. This lack of 'right manpower' made the company lag behind the market by many years. Had I started this industry in a metropolitan city like Chennai or Mumbai, I would have got the right manpower and I would have still helped my village by setting off a portion of the profit made by the company. This is a lesson I learned after establishing the company. While deciding the location, **Business Profit** alone must be the criterion.

Son: Thank you dad for sharing your experience. Finally, Valluvar has also spoken about 'Time'. Can you elaborate on this point?

Father: In today's business scenario, everything revolves around time. Starting a business is bound by a time period within which all the related activities of starting a business must be completed. For this, while implementing a project, the engineers draw a **PERT** chart called the **Program Evaluation Review Technique**. This PERT chart is a graph drawn on a horizontal time scale for various activities involved in implementing the project. Starting from the time of placing orders for the machinery, considering the 'lead time' for the machinery to arrive, their installation time, commissioning time, pilot lot production time etc., will be estimated and drawn on a time scale in the PERT chart. Using this PERT chart, all these activities will be monitored to ensure the completion of the project within the scheduled time.

Not only for starting the project, but also for all other activities like purchase, production, marketing, delivery etc. timely execution is important. Any business will be successful, only when the time schedule is adhered. Having understood the importance of 'time', Valluvar has added the time factor in this couplet.

In short, this couplet tells us comprehensively the important factors to be considered before starting a business. I have elaborated on these parameters for starting an industry. The details may vary for other businesses, though the elements to be considered remain the same. It is amazing, that a poet was able to visualize Modern Management Practices two thousand years back. His points are still valid and will be valid for years to come. This couplet is 'total and inclusive' and tells every entrepreneur to take all precautions and insists on absolute planning without assuming anything.

Any start-up entrepreneur, who adheres to this couplet will not face a failure and will be successful in the first attempt itself.

A wake-up call for start-ups!

------ •◦• ------

1.3 Couplet: 471 / Chapter: 48
Knowing the strength (வலியறிதல்)

வினைவலியும் தன்வலியும் மாற்றான் வலியும்
துணைவலியும் தூக்கிச் செயல்.

Accomplish a task by evaluating its toughness, own strength, opponent's strength and supporting strengths.

Son: Dad, Valluvar wants to be more cautious in business and that is why he wants to consider all the strengths before starting. Am I right?

Father: Yes. You are absolutely right. Valluvar does not want the king to fail in his war at any cost. Therefore he advocates a safer approach. The same philosophy applies to business also. No one should fail in business.

Son: Dad, What does Valluvar mean by the toughness of a mission or act?

Father: A mission can be any venture where there are challenges and competition. Here, I will consider the mission to be starting a new business. Toughness means the various factors of the business which affect its performance.

- Technology complexities.

- Process intricacies.

- Availability of raw materials (local or to be imported).

- Technical Standards compliances like DIN, NEMA etc.

- Adherences of quality compliances like ISO, CE, UL etc.

- Product approvals required like ALMM, ARAI, BIS etc.

- Safety certifications required if any.

- The requirement of After Sales Service.

- How much competition prevails? Is it severe?

- Whether the customers are 'quality conscious' or 'price conscious'?

- Availability of skilled manpower.

- The finance required to meet the above requirements.

- Government regulations to be complied.

- etc.

Like this many factors determine the toughness of the project. One must thoroughly evaluate the above points and understand the competencies (strengths) required.

Son: Dad, how to evaluate 'our own strength' in business?

Father: 'Our own strength' means readiness to meet the requirements listed above. One must evaluate whether he possesses all the competencies and infrastructure to meet the points listed above. If there are shortcomings he must improve and make himself eligible before venturing into business.

Son: What about competitors? They may have all these strengths.

Father: The competitor's strength in terms of the above parameters must be evaluated and a suitable action plan must be incorporated in our strategy to win over the competition. It may be a feature in the product, quality difference, price advantage or offering special service to customers. Wherever the shortfall is noticed on our side it must be addressed before entering the venture. At least one or two innovative features must be added to our product compared to the competitors. If the strengths are equal, establishing a good service network may be a good idea. Giving more warranty than the competitor will also help. All the decisions must focus on attracting the customers to our product.

Son: What does Valluvar mean by support strengths?

Father: Some competitors may have a strong technical tie-up or collaboration which makes a difference in customer perspective. Some companies may have a leading consulting company as their partners. Some companies may have strong political support. These additional supports give the end customers a belief or trust or a 'Brand Image'.

Son: Dad, can you explain to me about Brand Image?

Father: The brand is a market perception about a company or product derived over a period. The new companies may not have it. But they must spend substantial money on advertisements to create an impact in the market even before entering. Innovation in the product will break the brand of the competitors. I can give you the names of some companies, who entered the business without a brand name and created a brand in a short period.

In India **Ola Electric** was a new company without a brand name; but within a short time the company captured the market with innovations, huge advertisements and launch tactics. This has created a brand image for them.

Similarly, Amazon, Google, Facebook, Airbnb, Uber etc. are companies started without an earlier brand name and became brand leaders later.

Son: What exactly one should do after evaluating all these strengths?

Father: Wherever required one who starts a new venture must improve his 'own capabilities' to exceed or at least to match the strengths. Wherever possible, innovation must be deployed. A whole lot of work must be done to address every factor before entering into the market. The company must be able to prove its superiority over the competition. This is possible only when the strengths are evaluated (தூக்கிச் செயல்) as Valluvar says.

Son: Dad, I am thrilled by Valluvar's knowledge and I am very sure if someone reads this couplet will prepare well before venturing into any business.

Evaluate strengths before venturing!

1.4 Couplet: 462 / Chapter: 47
Knowledgeable Execution (தெரிந்துசெயல்வகை)

தெரிந்த இனத்தொடு தேர்ந்தெண்ணிச் செய்வார்க்கு
அரும்பொருள் யாதொன்றும் இல்.

No task is impossible to the one, who carefully selects the proper knowledge partner and performs.

Son: Dad, it seems Valluvar talks about keeping the right advisor; right?

Father: Yes. He talks of a knowledge partner. Business knowledge is very important to start a business. Everyone who starts a business may not possess all the knowledge required for a business. But, he may have finance, infrastructure and other requirements. For this reason, Valluvar recommends to choose a 'knowledge partner' who has the right experience in the similar line of activity (தெரிந்த இனத்தொடு) which is being pursued.

He is not recommending simply to appoint a knowledge partner. By using the Tamil word தேர்ந்தெண்ணி he means, thoroughly evaluate and select the partner. If such a competent partner or advisor is evaluated and tied up, according to Valluvar, it is possible to accomplish even rare tasks.

Many examples can be given for organisations that have tied up with competent companies and become successful.

In India, the biggest automobile manufacturer **Maruti selected Suzuki of Japan** as its knowledge partner. Because of this partnership, Maruti was able to become the top car manufacturing company in India and also to retain its position as number **one** in the market.

In the year 2004, the leading cycle manufacturing company **Hero** in India took **Honda of Japan** as its knowledge partner for manufacturing powered two-wheelers. This partnership has resulted in Hero becoming a top manufacturing company of powered two-wheelers in India.

Another good example of a successful business collaboration is the partnership between **Steve Jobs and Steve Wozniak**, co-founders of Apple. Their collaboration led to the creation of the **Apple I and Apple II** computers, which revolutionized the personal computer industry. Wozniak, an engineering genius, designed the hardware, while Steve Jobs, a visionary and marketing expert, handled the sales and marketing. Their complementary skills and shared passion for innovation led to the development of innovative products that transformed the computer industry.

Another good example is, **Amazon** becoming successful by acquiring **Whole Foods** to avail the advantage of its high-end grocery stores which existed across the country.

Globally, there are hundreds of companies, who have become very successful just because they have selected the right knowledge partner and collaborated with them. Therefore son, if you are entering a business in which you do not have full experience and knowledge, then, you MUST appoint an advisor or enter into collaboration with a company engaged in the same line of activity to offer you the know-how.

Have a knowledge partner and succeed!

1.5. Couplet: 461 / Chapter: 47
Knowledgeable Execution (தெரிந்துசெயல்வகை)

அழிவதூஉம் ஆவதூஉம் ஆகி வழிபயக்கும்
ஊதியமும் சூழ்ந்து செயல்.

Consider the income, the expenses and the resulting profit before venturing into a business.

Son: Dad, in this couplet, Valluvar talks of profit even before starting a business. Why?

Father: Yes. It is very important to know whether the business being planned will yield any profit before investing money. He says this must be arrived at by calculating the income, the expenses and the net profit which will arise out of this business. He wants a holistic consideration of all these parameters and to calculate the **Net Profit.**

Modern management advises us to prepare a **Project Report** before starting a business. Banks insist on a **Detailed Project Report (DPR)** to sanction a loan for a business. Both are, to ensure the profitability of the business.

Son: What is a Project Report?

Father: It is a document containing the investment details, possible income, expenses and the resulting profit. The P&L and Balance Sheet of the proposed project will also find a place in the Project Report. The Project Report is prepared by collecting the following data related to the proposed business.

- Various incomes possible from the business (Product Sales, Spare Parts Sales, Service Income etc.)

- The expenses like raw material cost, labour cost, electricity cost etc.

- The investment required (Land, Building, Machinery etc.)

- Working Capital required for running the business

- The Bank Loan required and the interest to be paid

From the above data, the expected profit will be calculated year-wise for five years. The **Break Even Point** which means the minimum sales required for zero profit is also calculated in this report to understand the project viability. The business can be started only when the project report shows the right profit for the investment made. Valluvar means that one should consider all the above parameters by using the Tamil word 'சூழ்ந்து செயல்' meaning considering holistically.

This is a very useful advice for young entrepreneurs who venture into new business initiatives.

Ensure profit before venturing!

1.6   Couplet: 758 / Chapter: 76
Ways of making wealth (பொருள்செயல்வகை)

குன்றேறி யானைப்போர் கண்டற்றால் தன்கைத்தொன்று
உண்டாகச் செய்வான் வினை.

Doing business with own funds is as easy as watching an 'elephants fight' from the top of a hill.

Son: Dad, this couplet is interesting because it talks of elephants fighting.

Father: Let us talk about elephants later. This couplet advocates doing business with own funds because it is free from hassles. From this couplet we can understand that in Valluvar's time also people used to borrow money for doing business. If not, Valluvar need not have written this couplet. The country in which Valluvar was living could have been so prosperous that many businesses were carried out in that country and the businessmen used to borrow money for their business.

During Valluvar's time, taking a loan was considered to be a socially unacceptable subject, because it led to worries. People were mostly honest and did not want to cheat. The character of the people was so good that a word given was as strong as signing in a bond paper. The mental stress one goes through for being answerable to return the dues 'on time' was felt very severely. Sometimes it went to the extent of affecting the business. Therefore, Valluvar has advised that doing business with 'own funds' would be free from stress. He was right.

Today, anyone who wants to start a business either borrows money from an individual or from a bank. Normally the interest rate is very high if borrowed from individuals. This is a big burden for business and a worrying point. The ordeal of getting a loan from a bank by filling up and submitting many documents, giving immovable properties as security, finding a chartered engineer to value the property etc. remains a significant task. More time has to be spent on carrying out all these formalities, which otherwise could be used to concentrate on business. In any case, borrowing is a stressful activity.

In spite of the above ordeals, today, we see many people borrowing loans from banks even if they are capable of meeting the investment with their own funds. There is an unwritten rule prevailing in the society, that anyone starting a business must get a bank loan. But, Valluvar differs. He says doing business with one's own funds is the easiest way of doing business.

To emphasize this point, Valluvar compares this to watching an 'elephants fight'. Normally it is not easy to watch elephants fighting in a forest. If you dare to watch from being close, then you put yourself at risk. The best way would be to watch it from the top of a hill so that you are away from the risks of the elephants harming you. Doing business with own funds is as easy as watching 'elephants fight' with ease, that is, from the top of a hill. Valluvar has given this example based on the events from his time. We should focus only on the point that he emphasizes through this interesting example, rather than the example itself.

Today, some people may not agree with the views of Valluvar. There may be arguments 'for and against' the point of doing business with own funds.

Son: What is your opinion, dad?

Father: Here, I leave the final decision to the individuals. I quote another couplet of Valluvar that helps in taking the right decision at this moment.

எப்பொருள் யார்யார்வாய்க் கேட்பினும் அப்பொருள்
மெய்ப்பொருள் காண்பது அறிவு. (குறள் - 423)

Irrespective of whoever has said a subject, it is wise to understand the truthful meaning of that subject. (Couplet - 423)

Here, Valluvar says one should not blindly accept everything he hears, even if it is told by the elders or the boss or by eminent personalities. He says, one must apply his mind and evaluate the subject, understand the reality and then decide. A great teaching by Valluvar. This teaching is applicable even to his teaching in the above couplet.

Own funds – worry less business!

1.7   Couplet: 473 / Chapter: 48
Know the Strength (வலியறிதல்)

உடைத்தம் வலியறியார் ஊக்கத்தின் ஊக்கி
இடைக்கண் முரிந்தார் பலர்.

Many have failed in between for starting out of emotional impulse without evaluating own strength.

Son: Dad, how can anyone start a business without knowing his own strength?

Father: It happens. In today's society, many people see others making big money by doing business. Naturally, these people, particularly youngsters are tempted to venture into some business after seeing other's success. In such situations, they see only their success and fail to see the strength possessed by them. Only for this reason, in India, 90% of the start-ups fail. The failure story is not explicitly known while the success stories are given wide publicity. This is a very important couplet by Valluvar. He says one must understand his 'own strength' before starting a venture.

In this couplet, Valluvar uses a Tamil word 'வலி'. This means Strength. The strength can be in terms of technical knowledge, managing capability, financial capability or any capability required to start a business. In management parlance, a terminology called SWOT analysis is used. This is an analysis to know one's strengths and weaknesses. Even the existing organisations periodically carry out this analysis to improve their inner strengths to achieve better business.

Son: Dad, this is very interesting. Can you explain the 'SWOT' analysis to me?

Father: SWOT analysis is a technique used to evaluate a company's strengths and weaknesses at any point of time. This can also be applied to an individual who wants to start a business. In 'SWOT' every letter has a meaning.

S - Strength

W - Weakness

O - Opportunity

T - Threat

Strength: Product knowledge, technology know-how, the market potential, availability of the relevant experienced staff, finance availability, the technical standards to be complied with and certifications to be obtained etc. If a person knows about all these aspects and is capable of meeting these requirements, then, he will be considered to be a strong and capable person to start a business.

Weakness: Shortcoming in any of the above aspects, is considered to be a weakness.

Opportunity: The growing market, export possibilities, incentives from the government etc. A person who starts a business must envisage these opportunities also.

Threat: Changing government policies, fluctuating exchange rates, growing competition, International political impact on the business being planned, possibilities of natural calamities etc. These kinds of threats to business must also be considered while taking a business decision.

The individual who wants to start a business must write down all his **strengths and weaknesses** and thoroughly analyse them, to understand his situation. After thorough analysis, wherever required he must improve his strengths. Also, he must eliminate weaknesses if any. If required he must engage knowledgeable consultants or experienced employees to make the SWOT analysis and make the net result of SWOT a 'positive one' before venturing into a business.

Valluvar says he has seen many people who have not done proper strength analysis as explained above (உடைத்தம் வலியறியார்) and started businesses out of emotional impulse (ஊக்கத்தின் ஊக்கி) failing in between.

Know yourself before venturing!

———•—

1.8.　Couplet: 760 / Chapter: 76
Means of making wealth (பொருள் செயல் வகை)

ஒண்பொருள் காழ்ப்ப இயற்றியார்க்கு எண்பொருள்
ஏனை இரண்டும் ஒருங்கு.

For those who do honest business, besides money,
virtuous life and eternal happiness will be bestowed.

Son: Dad, Valluvar advocates the honest way of doing business; right?

Father: Yes. Today, money is being earned in various ways. Some individuals make money only through honest ways, while others resort to dishonest ways. I have seen people who earn money through dishonest ways spending a portion of it on charities as a remedy. Still, such people will not be able to live a peaceful life. Valluvar insists on honest business practices. He says besides earning money, those who do honest business will enjoy a virtuous life and mental happiness.

Son: Dad, I am told that maintaining 100% honesty is not possible even if you wish to. Is that right?

Father: Yes son. This is true in a diversified society existing today. Honest people, doing business always face challenges in maintaining such honesty throughout. Sometimes they are forced to deviate from the principles to continue the business. Such occasions throw a question i-e whether to continue the business or not. For such a dilemma Valluvar has given a solution through another couplet of him.

பொய்மையும் வாய்மை யிடத்த புரைதீர்ந்த
நன்மை பயக்கும் எனின். (குறள் - 292).

Even a lie would take the place of truth,
if it brings blameless benefit. (Couplet - 292).

In this Couplet, Valluvar says that a lie is also acceptable, provided the lie results in a benefit to somebody without any kind of wrong motive either directly or indirectly.

This explanation will help people to conduct business without violating the moral principles of life. Valluvar is a down-to-earth philosopher, always preaching disciplines, which are practical and possible to follow in life. Many ascetics and saints of those days preached philosophies, which were pure, impeccable and absolute but failed in real life because those principles were very difficult to practice.

Ethical business earns money and virtues!

———•◦•———

1.9.   Couplet: 832 / Chapter: 84
Folly (பேதைமை)

பேதைமையுள் எல்லாம் பேதைமை காதன்மை
கையல்ல தன்கண் செயல்.

***It will be a folly among follies to involve in an act
about which one is not passionate.***

Son: Valluvar very strongly opposes anyone involving himself in any activity which he himself doesn't like.

Father: Yes. Valluvar is right. One should not undertake a job that does not suit his aptitude. This is the most important aspect of anyone's career and nowadays mostly ignored too.

Son: What happens if a person selects a job about which he is not passionate?

Father: The implications are invisible but manifold. These are not seen explicitly; but very intensive. Personally, it leads to dissatisfaction and unhappiness, low self-esteem and confidence, emotional exhaustion and feeling tired always. In addition, it develops a lack of interest in the job. In total, he will work with demotivation. Career-wise, it leads to failure.

Son: Understood dad. I find many of my friends who did not like the medical profession were forced to take up medical education by their parents. They have heeded the pressure and taken up the profession. Now what to do?

Father: Yes, it happens. In India, it prevails more. The only way is to offer substantial counselling and make them develop an aptitude for this career. Offering intensive training could be another way.

Son: Is this applicable for selecting a business also?

Father: I have seen people inheriting businesses from their parents or in-laws going through mental turmoil to run the business just because they do not like the business. This is also true when a new business is started. Either one should start a business which he likes or he must develop a passion for it after starting. Otherwise, his business performance will be greatly affected and will lead to a big failure.

In my own case, when I finished my first year of engineering in college, I was offered the civil engineering branch in the second year. I did not want to become a civil engineer because I was not passionate about it. I fought for the mechanical branch of engineering and finally got it. When I finished my engineering studies, immediately I got an offer for the post of 'Mechanical Draftsman' from a reputed company manufacturing boilers. Here again, I did not want to be a draftsman and I declined the offer. Later I joined the maintenance department of a process industry, a role which I liked. In both of the above cases, I was very firm that I would not accept a career that I did not like. Today I am happy about those decisions.

If you do not like an act, do not indulge!

Summing up the messages given above,

- Be passionate about the business you want to start.

- Start with the help of a suitable knowledge partner.

- Start with a proper Project Report

- Ensure that the business will make profit.

- Start preferably with own funds.

- Conduct a SWOT analysis before starting.

- Choose the right product, location, process and machinery and meet the time schedules.

- Follow honesty in business.

Great advices from a great poet on starting a business!

VALLUVAR'S GUIDANCE
TO
A MANAGING DIRECTOR / CEO

2.0 To the MD / CEO

Son: Dad, what kind of advice Valluvar has given to the Managing Director or CEO of today?

Father: Valluvar has given a lot of suggestions to a king for successfully managing his empire. These are mainly for safeguarding his country from enemies and keeping his citizens happy. Surprisingly, all these ideas given by him to a king have become very relevant for today's Business Management also.

Son: Is it? It is quite interesting. Can you briefly explain what exactly he has written to help today's Managing Director or CEO?

Father: Running an industry or business is not an easy task. It is more difficult to manage it continuously and to sustain it. A CEO or Managing Director requires multiple skill sets to manage a business. He has to manage the various departments of an industry from Purchase to Sales, including Production, Quality, Finance, Marketing, Commercial, Customer support, Research and Development, etc. Above all, he has to comply with the government rules and regulations, both domestic and international. Unless he has certain unique capabilities, he cannot manage an industry effectively.

Though Valluvar has not given a complete solution for the competencies required, he has understood these requirements and brought out certain general management codes and ideas in his couplets. These codes talk about the attitude required for a business leader. We can say that these teachings will change the personality of a CEO and make him more competent. Now, let us see some of the ideas given by Valluvar to a CEO.

2.1   Couplet: 547 / Chapter: 55
Justice (செங்கோன்மை)

இறைகாக்கும் வையகம் எல்லாம் அவனை
முறைகாக்கும் முட்டாச் செயின்.

***A king will safeguard his country, but he will be safeguarded
by the uninterrupted systems created by him.***

Son: Dad, I can understand the statement that a king will safeguard his country. But, how can the systems created by him will save him? It sounds irrelevant!

Father: No. Valluvar never says irrelevant things. I will give some examples from today's management. Once you read this, you will appreciate Valluvar's contention.

Today, a CEO has to manage many departments under him, right from purchase to marketing. Every department carries out different activities to achieve its goal. The CEO can't manage all the departments directly, because every department's function will be different and vast. To manage these day-to-day activities without his presence, every activity is visualized and a working procedure is created and documented by him. This documented procedure is called a **"Standard Operating Procedure - SOP"**. This SOP will be written for all the possible activities of all the departments. Everyone in the department will be trained to follow these procedures meticulously. If any unforeseen situation arises that deviates from the SOP, a deviation handling procedure is also incorporated in the SOP, so that, the process never stops. Every time a new challenge is faced, a solution is given by the management and also incorporated into the SOP through proper amendments.

Over a period, the SOP becomes a very strong tool that runs the organisation without the daily involvement of the CEO. The CEO can operate from a remote location. This means the system created by him takes care of him.

Son: That sounds interesting Dad! Any example for this?

Father: Yes. Many examples can be given. I will give you a few.

You know **Tata Group** in India. They have many companies operating in India and abroad. The chairman of the group, **Mr. Ratan Tata** (who passed away when this book is being written) used to sit in Mumbai and manage all the companies. How? All the companies of Tata Group follow similar systems for their day-to-day operations and his presence was not necessary in any of his companies. **The systems created by him took care of him**.

You must have visited the **Apollo Hospital** in Chennai where many hundreds of patients are offered treatment in a day. Right from the registration of the patients, directing them to the appropriate doctor, getting all the tests done, getting the reports and meeting the doctor for the final prescription etc. are managed through proper systems and procedures. This enables the patients to get treatment without any hassle. Only because of these flawless systems, this hospital can handle hundreds of patients in a day and also carry out a record number of cardiac surgeries in a day. All these things are done without the involvement of the CEO of the hospital on a daily basis.

McDonald's standardized procedures all over the world ensure consistency in food quality and customer experience making the brand a great success. Here also the systems take care of the business owner.

Amazon: Their efficient logistics and supply chain management systems enable fast and reliable delivery and are the key to the success.

Rotary Club, Lion's Club and **BNI** kind of social organisations are also successful only because of their strong systems.

Many more examples can be given to prove this statement.

Son: Dad, Valluvar uses the word called "முட்டாச் செயின்" in this couplet. What does it mean?

Father: You got the right point. Valluvar's vocabulary in Tamil is fabulous. He uses words that no other poet has used. This kind of usage also displays the strength of Tamil as a language. The word "முட்டாச் செயின்" means "uninterrupted" in English. Valluvar says the systems created by the organisation must be so foolproof that it does not face any interruption. This is because the system consists of a chain of activities and every activity must be completed following a particular procedure within the stipulated time. If any part of the chain breaks or gets stuck, the whole system fails. Let us take the example of Apollo Hospitals once again. Here all the functions of handling the patients are digitally managed using computers and special software. If any computer fails or software crashes in any particular stage of the process, it will affect the flow of the process and the patients will get stuck at that point and will suffer. To avoid this, the management has taken many steps to ensure the systems and the networks are managed well to work without any interruption. This is one of the reasons for the success of the hospital. Therefore it is not only the system, but the **uninterrupted** system which is essential. Valluvar has emphasized this point in this couplet.

Son: Dad, you told me that the systems can be common for many industries or businesses. Can't we develop a common system so that all industries can follow it?

Father: There are many software solutions available today called **ERP (Enterprise Resource Planning).** These ERPs have the required general systems developed and programmed for running a business. The ERP-implementing companies will use their general template and tailor it to suit the requirements of a particular industry. Today many companies have started using ERPs to automate their business processes to save time and increase productivity.

Flawless systems - Endless benefits!

2.2   couplet: 512 / Chapter: 52
Knowledgeable Performance (தெரிந்து வினையாடல்)

வாரி பெருக்கி வளம்படுத் துற்றவை
ஆராய்வான் செய்க வினை.

***Let the one who brings in various sources of income,
adds resources and handles the hurdles, manage.***

Son: Dad, Can you explain the meaning of this couplet?

Father: This couplet talks of Business Development of an existing business, because, no business can be static. While the existing business is doing well one should think of additional income possibilities.

Son: Why dad? What is the problem in continuing only with the existing business when it is doing well?

Father: When the business is doing well, many competitors may emerge over a period of time. This will force the company to reduce the prices in the market and naturally, the profit will start eroding. The salaries of the existing employees may go up over a period. Other expenses and overheads will increase because of inflation. All these factors will lead to a reduction in profit, and in the long run, may lead to losses also. This must be foreseen by the management and new sources of income must be explored as a precautionary measure. Therefore **'continuous business development'** is a must to sustain any business. Valluvar makes this point through this couplet.

Son: Which is better? Starting a new business or to find out ways and means of expanding the existing business?

Father: In this couplet, Valluvar means the ways and means of increasing the income from the existing business only. In today's scenario, there are many ways of approaching this. I will list a few here.

1. Marketing the **spare parts** of the main products. A smart management can package its spares in such a way that it fetches additional revenues.

2. If there is a novelty in the existing business, selling the novel idea to others will bring additional business. (**Technology Transfer**)

3. Offering **new features** in the existing products and increasing the prices to get additional revenue. (Most car companies follow this strategy to increase their revenue)

4. Resorting to **'In-House Manufacturing'** of some of the 'Bought Out' parts to reduce the cost.

5. Opening **small manufacturing units** for the same products in vantage locations to reduce freight expenses.

Therefore, trying to identify the areas of additional income using the same knowledge and facilities will increase the sustainability of the business.

Son: Why does Valluvar talk of 'resources' in this couplet?

Father: Here resources means infrastructure. It is not simply looking for new avenues of income. The new idea may require certain infrastructure like machinery, processes, space, power etc. This must be thought of and 'Return on Investment' has to be calculated and ensured.

Son: Valluvar talks of 'hurdles' in this couplet. What kind of hurdles?

Father: Any additional income possibility is like an additional business avenue. This requires careful planning and envisaging the hurdles and solutions thereof. Valluvar says careful decisions are important while looking at additional revenues to mitigate any risk.

Son: Why Valluvar has used the word 'ஆராய்வான்' in this couplet?

Father: All the points mentioned above like new business avenues, creating infrastructure and eliminating possible risks cannot be implemented without thorough evaluation. Every parameter must be explored with relevant data and decided. It is like doing a research work. It must be within the ambit of the existing business capabilities. Finally, this additional business must result in good profit, for which thorough analysis is required. This is meant by Valluvar by using the above word '**ஆராய்வான்**'.

Son, Valluvar says that a manager who is capable of evaluating and implementing all these factors alone can accomplish this.

Enhance the existing business and earn more!

2.3 Couplet: 385 / Chapter: 39
The glory of a king (இறை மாட்சி)

இயற்றலும் ஈட்டலும் காத்தலும் காத்த
வகுத்தலும் வல்லது அரசு.

A competent kingdom devises avenues of income, collects, safeguards and apportions appropriately.

Son: Dad, what is the message Valluvar is trying to communicate in this couplet?

Father: Valluvar talks of additional income possibilities which we have already seen in the previous couplet. He also talks of protecting such income earned and apportioning it for different useful activities of the business. This is called **'Budgeting'** in today's management.

Valluvar also indicates the revenue through such ways must be properly collected (ஈட்டலும்) without any dues. Today, many companies offer credit sales to customers. This becomes inevitable under severe competitive situations. However, collection and recovery of the dues are important and such dues must be collected without any write-offs. In today's business, collecting the dues after supplying the product is always tough. In international business, it is highly risky. For this reason, most of the Chinese companies do not offer any credit to customers. Instead, they offer a better price and take the full payment before effecting the supply.

If a 'credit sales' is entertained, there are some methods like a Letter of Credit (LC), Bank Guarantee etc. followed by the banks through which the banks ensure the payment to the supplier. The bank will charge a fee for this operation. Valluvar says to collect the dues without fail and one can follow any of the above methods.

Valluvar also advocates safeguarding such earnings from unnecessary expenses and advises suitable budgeting of the expenses with proper apportionment. He uses the word 'வகுத்தலும்' which means apportioning of the income for useful purposes.

Normally the companies use a certain percentage of the Reserves and Surplus funds for buying additional machinery to increase production, improve quality etc. Some companies spend a percentage on employee welfare. According to Valluvar a competent CEO does all these planning.

Budget the funds and manage the finances!

2.4 Couplet: 520 / Chapter: 52
Knowledgeable Performance (தெரிந்து வினையாடல்)

நாடோறும் நாடுக மன்னன் வினைசெய்வான்
கோடாமை கோடாது உலகு.

A country will never go down if the king ensures motivation of his functionaries as a matter of daily routine.

Son: Dad, I think Valluvar talks of motivation in this couplet. Does he talk about the motivation of his citizens or functionaries (employees) in the government?

Father: Since he has used the word 'விளை செய்வான்' he means the functionaries of the government only. If the functionaries are kept motivated, naturally, they take care of the citizens.

This applies to the employees of today's organisations as well. Valluvar emphasizes that 'employee happiness' is very important and according to him, the CEO must watch this on a daily basis. Happiness leads to motivation. Motivation leads to high performance. Statistics say that a motivated employee's productivity is higher by 25% than a normal employee. Also, a motivated employee produces 25% better quality products. Employee retention of motivated employees are higher by 45%.

Having understood this point, the HR department today spends a lot of money in keeping the employees motivated. The main job of this department is to promote many motivational schemes for the employees and keep them happy always. A separate budget is earmarked for this purpose by the company. The HR department spends this budget in various motivational schemes to benefit the employees. All these measures will result in **"Total Employee Involvement"** in the organisation. If this is achieved the company's performance will improve many fold.

Son: Dad, What are the factors that may cause demotivation among employees?

Father: Demotivation among employees arises out of improper HR policies.

- The employees compare their salary with their colleagues and expect equality in salaries among the same grade in employment. If there is a discrepancy, the affected employee gets demotivated. If for any reason, one employee has to be given better pay, it must be justified and must be acceptable to everyone.

- Favouritism by the management leads to demotivation among employees.

- If a good work done by an employee is not recognized, it leads to demotivation.

- When an employee faces any major problem at home, he expects a personal touch from the management. If not given it leads to demotivation.

Son: What happens when demotivation prevails in an organisation?

Father: Demotivation is highly infectious. It spreads easily to other employees. It spoils the morality of the company and affects the production. The product quality may suffer. Timely Delivery will be affected. In total, it affects the entire organisation.

Son, for the above reasons, Valluvar advises the top man of the organisation to continuously ensure that the employees are free from any kind of demotivation. According to him, if this is ensured, the organisation will not go down.

Take care of the employees - they will take care of you!

2.5 Couplet: 1022 / Chapter: 103
Uplifting the citizens (குடி செயல் வகை)

ஆள்வினையும் ஆன்ற அறிவும் எனஇரண்டின்
நீள்வினையான் நீளும் குடி.

Enhancement of both skill and insightful knowledge will lead to enhanced livelihood of the citizens.

Son: Dad, It seems Valluvar is referring to knowledge and competency in this couplet.

Father: This couplet reminds me of a popular saying. Instead of providing fish curry food to a needy person, teach him the technique of catching fish. The best way to tackle poverty is to provide skills which will enable an individual to earn. In those days, when employment opportunities were not available in their country, people used to migrate to other countries searching for jobs to meet their livelihood. To prevent this, Valluvar proposes giving extended skill and extra knowledge to them. If such measures are taken, their competency increases, which leads to more local job opportunities reducing their need to leave their country (minimizing attrition). When he says extended knowledge, he means imparting additional knowledge over and above what they possess now. If the people are given such extended knowledge in skill and execution, some of them may start their own businesses locally and create job opportunities for others. A country which has more educated and knowledgeable people will have more business opportunities that make the country stronger and more powerful. Today, countries like the US, Japan, and Germany prove this statement. The people of these countries do not seek employment abroad.

In today's business, the management uses this idea of offering extra knowledge to its employees to reduce attrition. Many initiatives are taken to offer soft skill development to their employees. It is done both in-house and outside the organisation. The employees are deputed to various seminars to increase their competency. The management allots a substantial budget for this. This makes employees more proficient in their job and feels secure in the organisation.

In the fast-developing business world, every faculty of management undergoes changes and new ideas like Artificial Intelligence are emerging every day. The employees need to stay updated on these developments. Otherwise, the organisation will fall behind its competitors. This is another reason why the extended knowledge of employees becomes essential.

Valluvar mentions managing knowledge and domain knowledge (ஆள்வினையும் ஆன்ற அறிவும்) distinctly in this couplet, because both are equally important for successfully executing any assignment. According to Valluvar, this kind of knowledge enhancement makes the employees get more involved in the organisation's goals and eventually results in employee retention. (less attrition).

I heard that, Mr.Narayanamurthy, the former CEO of Infosys, used to attend training at his training center for a few days in a year. This was to keep himself updated on the latest developments in technology and management. This proves that such knowledge development is required for CEOs also.

Son: Dad, Why should the organisation worry about manpower retention? If someone leaves, it can always get candidates from outside, right?

Father: You are wrong. Experience is the most important competency of an employee. If an experienced employee leaves, it may take a lot of time to train a newcomer in his place. Sometimes, it may be difficult to get the right candidate for the replacement. This leads to time and money loss. Therefore every organisation strives hard to retain its existing manpower at any cost. The loss of revenue arising out of losing an experienced employee and recruiting a new employee is a 'deceptive loss'. It may not reflect directly, but there will be a substantial loss.

One more point. Today's youngsters, even though they are well paid, they leave the organisation if the scope for such knowledge development is not available in the present organisation. They value their knowledge growth more than their salary.

Enrich employee skills - eliminate attrition!

2.6 Couplet: 582 / Chapter: 59
Espionage (ஒற்றாடல்)

எல்லார்க்கும் எல்லாம் நிகழ்பவை எஞ்ஞான்றும்
வல்லறிதல் வேந்தன் தொழில்.

It is the duty of a king always to know thoroughly about all the happenings happening around him.

Son: Dad, can you explain this Couplet to me?

Father: If a king has to rule his country effectively, he must get to know the various happenings in his own country and as well in other countries. For this reason, on those days, the kings used to depute spies everywhere to gather information and report back to them. Since this is a very important activity, Valluvar has written one full chapter on 'Espionage' in Thirukkural. In this chapter, he describes how a spy should function and collect information. This information is vital for the king to take his day-to-day decisions and such decisions decide the fate of his country.

It is equally important for today's CEO to get as much data as possible about the market, the competitors, new technology etc. to make the best of the decisions to run his business.

Son: I think 'taking the right decision' is the implied meaning of this couplet. Am I right dad?

Father: Yes. Decision-taking is very important in business and also in one's personal life. Every individual takes decisions at every moment in his life. If the decisions taken by an individual are correct, then, he becomes successful in his life. A study says, if a person can take seven out of ten decisions correctly, then, he becomes a successful man, because nobody can take 100% of their decisions correctly. People, who take four to six successful decisions out of ten, end up with average success. People who take less than four decisions correctly become unsuccessful in life. These people generally blame **'fate'** without realizing the fact that they have taken more wrong decisions. Let us assume that a person is highly educated, but takes mostly wrong decisions. Naturally, he ends up as a failure in life. On the contrary, a person who is 'less educated', but takes mostly the right decisions, becomes successful in life. Unfortunately, the society brands him as **'Lucky'**. Son, mark my words....

"A man's success at any point of time in his life is the net effect of all the decisions taken by him till then"

This is more relevant for today's Managing Director or CEO who takes decisions every moment in his business. To take correct decisions, he requires various data on all areas of his business. Realizing this fact, Valluvar recommends that a CEO (king) must get to know all the happenings around him continuously.

Son: So dad, what kind of data does a CEO require for his day-to-day decisions?

Father: Well. I will tell you some important areas in which a CEO requires regular information, though, in reality, much more data may be required. It varies depending on the type of business.

- Market conditions and fluctuations
- Competitor Movements
- Changing Technologies
- Innovations in his field
- Changing Government Policies and Taxations
- Employee Performance
- Employee Satisfaction
- Key employee attrition possibilities
- Employee skill and knowledge levels
- etc.

The CEO must be continuously aware of all the above happenings in his organisation. That is why Valluvar has used the word "எஞ்ஞான்றும்" which means 'always'.

Son: Is it the only way available to take decisions? I mean, decisions through data? No other way?

Father: There are many other ways too. An experienced person's **intuition** will tell what is right or what is wrong. Intuition-based decisions are highly subjective and depend on the person who takes the decisions. **Learning from other's experiences** is another way of taking decisions. **Consulting the experts** in this field is also a prevailing method. The best way is to collect data, analyze and discuss them in business **meetings** and decide the further course of action. Decisions taken in a meeting room are mostly correct and successful.

Son: Dad, How do we get this data? Where are they available?

Father: In today's modern world, a lot of avenues are prevailing to get these information. One must use these avenues to get such information.

- Internet

- Exhibitions (National and International)

- Seminars

- Knowledge sharing Training Sessions

- Books, Journals etc.

- Competitor information gathered by the travelling marketing and service team

- By joining the organisations like CII, FICCI, Linked IN etc.

- Networking with industry comrades

- Social media and WhatsApp

Son: Dad! Valluvar has used a word "வல்லறிதல்" in this couplet. What does it mean?

Father: The information collected from the above sources may not be always true. There are possibilities of distorted information and wrong data. For this reason, Valluvar has used the above special word which means, **check thoroughly, verify and understand the correctness of the data.** If not, the decisions taken based on these wrong data will be wrong and will have serious consequences on business. There is no meaning in taking a wrong decision and repenting later.

Son! Keeping all the above points in mind, Valluvar says that a CEO must get to know all the happenings around him regularly. Though Valluvar has used only seven words in this couplet, the meaning is elaborate and very important for today's business whether big or small.

Right information leads to right decisions!

2.7 Couplet: 584 / Chapter: 59
Espionage (ஒற்றாடல்)

வினைசெய்வார் தம்சுற்றம் வேண்டாதார் என்றாங்கு
அனைவரையும் ஆராய்வது ஒற்று.

The job of a spy is not only to watch the enemies but also to monitor the subordinates and relatives of the king.

Son: Dad, why does Valluvar suspect everyone around a king? Does it mean a CEO of today must also be suspicious of everyone around him?

Father: You're young; there's still a lot of time to gain experience. In today's business, the competitors are in no way less dangerous than the enemies of the kings in the past. These competitors want to win in the market by weakening the other. Normally, the CEO is very busy in managing the business and he may overlook certain things happening within the organisation. This is especially true in the case of medium and large-scale companies where the CEO has limited time to get to know about everything happening around him. Under severe competitive environments, the competitors may try to poach the best manpower, but the company cannot afford to lose them. Therefore the CEO must remain vigilant regarding his subordinates. The company may be developing new products that require secrecy till it is released to the market or a patent is obtained. This requires vigilance to safeguard the technology under development. Some companies have relatives as partners or directors. In such companies, some family problems might arise, which may lead to enmity in the board. The CEO must be careful about these factors.

I have seen employees betraying their own organisation even for small lapses in management. This is because the employees think the organisation is too big and should not commit even a small mistake. This kind of attitude prevails in industries today. Even a small discrepancy in the salary is not accepted. They expect a very fair treatment from the management. Particularly the promotions given to others create demotivation among some employees and such demotivation leads to unhappiness. These unhappy employees sometimes go to the extent of passing on certain vital information to the competitors.

Therefore, a CEO must be watchful of such possibilities. In big organisations certain trustworthy employees are kept to inform such harmful developments on time.

Valluvar is always practical and understands the complacency situation of a CEO and advises him to be watchful.

Watch everyone around including the favoured!

2.8 Couplet: 588 / Chapter: 59
Espionage (ஒற்றாடல்)

ஒற்றுஒற்றித் தந்த பொருளையும் மற்றுமோர்
ஒற்றினால் ஒற்றிக் கொளல்.

A king must verify and validate the information
got by one spy using another spy.

Son: Dad, Why is Valluvar so pessimistic and wants even the information brought by the king's own spy to be verified? Is it relevant to today's management?

Father: Yes. It's very relevant. There is a saying. **"When you are on top, you are alone"**, meaning, the top man of an organisation keeps himself at a distance from others. He cannot be close to anyone. Therefore, people under him hesitate to pass on even important information to him. Many times I too have realised this point. Using this situation, occasionally, his own subordinates might give twisted information to please him. Particularly, some executives from the marketing department, in the interest of proving that they know more than their colleagues, may pass on wrong market information. Similarly, there are many chances for incorrect information from other departments to reach the CEO.

Apart from the above, in today's condition, many fake messages circulate on WhatsApp and other social media. They often appear to be truthful information but actually, they are fake messages. This also requires verification before taking any action based on these messages.

Considering all these possibilities of misinformation, the CEO must have a mechanism in place to ensure the correctness of these messages before taking any decision. Otherwise, the decision taken based on wrong information can lead to costly mistakes. Instead of repenting, it is better to be cautious and employ someone to verify the truth, particularly on the subjects based on which critical decisions are taken.

Verify all the information even from reliable sources!

2.9 Couplet: 445 / Chapter: 45
Taking the support of elders (பெரியாரைத் துணைக்கோடல்)

சூழ்வார் கண்ணாக ஒழுகலான் மன்னவன்
சூழ்வாரைச் சூழ்ந்து கொளல்.

A king must be surrounded by good advisors since he sees the world through them.

Son: Dad, Is it necessary for the CEO to keep someone around him to be successful?

Father: Many times, the CEO requires some trustworthy person around him to critically assess the subject from all angles and advise him. This person will help the top man in taking crucial decisions. Sometimes a lower level subordinate might have valid information to pass on. But, hesitation will prevent him from going to the top man. If an intermediate person is available around the top man, the message can be passed on through him. The person around the CEO will act as a bridge for others to approach the top man.

Besides gathering information, the top man needs someone around him who can openly discuss certain ideas without fear or hesitation. This will help him to take the right decisions. Such people must also be talented and knowledgeable to have meaningful discussions particularly when the key decisions require careful deliberation. If a decision is taken with proper discussion, the chances of it failing are very low. Valluvar has visualized these situations and suggests keeping the right person around the CEO.

Son: Very interesting Dad! Does this really happen in practice?

Father: Yes. I can give a few examples. I am sure you are aware that Reliance is a very big group in India. There is one **Mr. Manoj Modi** who is very close to **Mr. Mukesh Ambani**, the CEO, who helps him in taking decisions. Mr.Manoj Modi played a key role in many of Mr.Mukesh Ambani's business decisions, including the successful investment of Rs.43000/-crores (5000 Million USD) in JIO. Even now, Mr. Manoj Modi helps the successors of Mr. Mukesh Ambani in business.

I can give you another example.

Mr. Warren Buffet is the CEO of Berkshire Hathaway, a king in the share market business and an expert in investments. Do you know that he too had a close associate around him to help him in taking the right decisions? His name is **Charlie Munger** and he was the Vice Chairman of Berkshire. He also had a business for himself, but worked very closely with Warren Buffet, providing support to him in terms of investment insights, strategic investments, leadership and business operations. He shares Warren Buffet's success story.

A few more examples are:

- Steve Jobs and Joanna Hoffman **(Apple)**,

- Bill Gates and Lisa Brummel **(Microsoft)**

- Mark Zuckerberg and Chris Cox **(Facebook)**

Valluvar was right. Many successful businessmen had some supporting persons to help them. Valluvar had understood the importance of having the right person for support and he had carefully chosen the phrase "keeping around".

Have the right advisors around!

2.10 Couplet: 448 / Chapter: 45
Taking the support of elders (பெரியாரைத் துணைக் கோடல்)

இடிப்பாரை இல்லாத ஏமரா மன்னன்
கெடுப்பார் இலானுங் கெடும்.

***A king not having a critic around him doesn't require
anyone else to spoil him; he will get spoiled on his own.***

Son: Dad, why does Valluvar insist on having someone who can criticize the CEO?

Father: Whoever it is or whichever position he occupies, one cannot always take the right decision unless someone is around him to help in taking right decisions. It will be much better if the person around him happens to be a critic. Decisions taken without discussions or criticism have a higher chance of failing.

That's why in the previous couplet Valluvar emphasized the point of having some competent person around the CEO. In this couplet, he specifically suggests that this person should also be a constructive critic. He warns that the king who doesn't have such a critic does not require anyone else to spoil him, because he will get spoiled by his own unilateral decisions.

In today's democratic political systems, it may not be practically possible to have a critic around the top man who rules a country. But, if he listens to the constructive criticisms from the opposition parties, he will commit fewer mistakes. Unfortunately, in today's democratic setup, rulers often do not listen to criticisms from the opposition, and it is also a fact that the opposition does not make constructive criticisms. A real leader of a nation should foster a culture of neutrality and encourage constructive feedback from the opposition.

Coming to today's business scenario, it may be difficult for a CEO to have a critic around him. Nevertheless, he still needs constructive criticism to improve his decisions. For this, he can judiciously use the 'meetings' conducted by him. He can encourage his team during meetings to offer constructive feedback to help improve his decisions. Many CEOs today do not allow their team members to voice their opinions. Because of this, the decisions taken in a meeting get passed without any deliberations and on many occasions, face failure. If given a free hand, the participants in a meeting might offer a range of varied and tangential comments. These comments are often surprisingly accurate and add value to the subject being discussed. Therefore, let us take the essence of this couplet to encourage constructive criticism and refine the decisions to achieve success in business.

Welcome criticisms – Improve the decisions!

2.11 Couplet: 447 / Chapter: 45
Taking the support of elders (பெரியாரைத் துணைக்கோடல்)

இடிக்கும் துணையாரை ஆள்வாரை யாரே
கெடுக்கும் தகைமை யவர்?

*"Who can spoil a king who knows how to handle
the critics around him?"*

Son: Dad, Valluvar says the king must have a critic. I agree. Why does he say that the critic must be handled carefully?

Father: That's a good question. The moment you allow a person to be your advisor, naturally, you are cut off from the subordinates. Subordinates find it convenient to approach the advisor and give their suggestions. Over a period, the advisor will start getting a feeling that the king will accept whatever he says and he may mislead the king for his own benefit. Also, he will start giving decisions to the subordinates on behalf of the king without even consulting the king. Such advisors may hide certain critical information from the king.

For the above reasons, the king must handle the critics carefully in such a way that the critic's knowledge is utilized, but at the same time, he does not fall into the traps of the critic.

Similarly, in today's management, a CEO must be very careful about his close associates in handling suggestions in the meetings. It must be an inbuilt trait for the CEO to discern between good and bad advice without being carried away by illusions. This requires an extraordinary sense, which, if not already present, a CEO must develop.

In short, Valluvar says that every CEO must have advisors and at the same time must know how to handle them.

Have critics around - handle them with care!

2.12 Couplet: 889 / Chapter: 89
Internal enmity (உட்பகை)

எட்பக வன்ன சிறுமைத்தே ஆயினும்
உட்பகை உள்ளதாங் கேடு.

However tiny the internal enmity be
it is dangerous.

Son: Is this couplet applicable for today's organisations also? Is it possible to have such enmity in the organisations?

Father: Yes. It is possible. Jealousy among the top management team is common nowadays. This jealousy creates enmity. Dissatisfaction during promotion turns into enmity. Under a severely competitive environment, the competitor companies may play a role in creating enmity within the organisation. When the HR policy of a company is anti-employee, naturally enmity breeds. Outsiders intruding amongst workmen and instigating them against the management is a major cause of enmity in the manufacturing sector.

Son: That sounds dangerous. How to tackle it?

Father: The management must be very vigilant about these factors and must eliminate them at the budding stage itself. That is why, in one of the earlier couplets, Valluvar has said that the CEO must get to know things happening around him always. The root cause of enmity must be identified and corrective action must be taken. Those elements causing internal enmity must be removed from the organisation. However, counseling and compromising efforts will also yield results.

Son: Dad, have you faced any such situation in your organisation?

Father: Yes son. One day, my personal secretary came to my room and told me that the attitude of some of the workmen was not good and they were instigating other good employees against the management. I didn't take it seriously and I was complacent. I told her not to imagine too much because our employees are good people and will never indulge in such activities. But, she was right. It was actually the handwork of some outsiders with political background, who instigated the workmen against the management. This led to a major labour issue that took me five years of court battles to resolve. The lesson learned was, as Valluvar says, even a small enmity should never be allowed to prolong in an organisation.

Have an eye on internal enmity!

------◆------

2.13 Couplet: 653 / Chapter: 66
Purity in Performance (வினைத் தூய்மை)

ஓஓதல் வேண்டும் ஒளிமாழ்கும் செய்வினை
ஆஅது என்னு மவர்.

One who aspires a great position in life will not indulge in acts that will spoil his credibility.

Son: Very important advice by Valluvar.

Father: Getting a good name in society does not happen in one day or based on a single event. It comes over years of being successful and notable. But this gathered name over a period can get spoiled by one mistake. It will spoil the entire name earned over years in a day.

In business, a brand name is built over the years based on quality products, timely service and more than everything, following honest business practices. Some factors which add to the credibility of the organisation are paying the employee salary on time, government taxes on time, suppliers' payments on time, maintaining the product quality and offering timely after-sales service etc. In India, Tata Group, HCL Technologies and Infosys are some examples.

However, there are a few companies which lost their brand names and credibility because of some wrong deeds. A few examples are Sathyam Group in India involved in a share manipulation scandal, Jet Airways involved in a financial scandal etc. These companies had a big reputation and the name got spoiled because of scandals.

Valluvar warns the reputed business people to desist from acts that will bring discredit to them. This is also applicable to aspiring entrepreneurs who want to grow.

Avoid discrediting acts if a credit-worthy life is aspired!

Summing up the messages given above,

- The importance of 'SOP' in an organisation

- Cash Flow Management

- Continuous improvement

- Keeping employee happiness at the forefront

- Employee retention

- Information gathering and its importance

- Collecting the correct Information

- Keeping the right people around

- Why to keep critics around and how to manage such critics

- Vigilance in management

- Handling internal enmity

- Sustaining credibility to achieve heights

Great thoughts!

Not only in Life Science but also in Management Science!

VALLUVAR'S ADVICE
TO
A MANAGER

3.0 The role of a Manager in an organisation

Son: Dad! What is the difference between the functional requirements of a CEO and a Manager?

Father: The responsibility of running an organisation lies with the CEO and he has to manage the various departments like Production, R&D, Purchase, Sales etc. As a single person, he cannot handle all these departments and hence he appoints managers to manage every department. Each manager has to manage the supervisors and other employees under him. The duty of successfully running a department lies in the hands of a manager and the competencies required for him are more towards managing the functional and process requirements of a department, while the CEO has to manage the policies, finance and inter-departmental coordination. Every manager has to run his department efficiently ensuring utmost productivity. If all the managers ensure this, the whole organisation will function successfully. The managers require in-depth knowledge of the technology and process and also must be good in interpersonal relationships. The manager must be a highly responsible person and has to lead his subordinates to achieve the target of his department. Now let us see some couplets written by Valluvar for the managers.

3.1.　Couplet: 631 / Chapter: 64
Ministry (அமைச்சு)

கருவியும் காலமும் செய்கையும் செய்யும்
அருவினையும் மாண்டது அமைச்சு.

A good ministry outperforms even impossible tasks by deploying the right tool, right method, at the right time.

Son: Dad, I think Valluvar talks about the correct way of executing a job by a manager. Am I right?

Father: Yes. You are right. Though the word 'அமைச்சு' in this couplet means 'Ministry', in management parlance it means the 'management'. Valluvar says if a manager deploys the correct tools (machinery), keeps up the time schedule, maintains the process of executing the task and if it is a special task understands the nature of the specialty, then he can successfully carry out even impossible tasks.

Here Valluvar uses a Tamil word 'செய்கை'. This word does not simply mean an act or task. It means the complete process of executing a task from start to end. Valluvar says the manager must understand thoroughly the entire process of executing a task.

Next Valluvar uses a word 'காலம்'. A simple meaning of this word is 'Time'. The job being executed may consist of many sub-activities like material procurement, inspection, manufacturing, quality control, delivery etc. Every activity has to be completed in a certain time frame and Valluvar says that a manager must control the time parameters of all these activities.

Next, he says, the correct tool or machinery must be chosen to carry out the above process and within the specified time. The tool may be a physical machine, virtual software or a combination of both.

Valluvar uses another word 'அருவினை' meaning rare jobs or special jobs. In case the job being planned is a rare job involving high-tech processes, then, the manager must understand the specialty of the job and accordingly he must choose the process and the machinery.

Son: Dad, Can you give me some practical examples for this Couplet?

Father: Yes. I can quote **Swiggy** and **Amazon** as typical examples of rare jobs. These two businesses involve a tremendous amount of process. Right from registering the requirement of a customer, defining the logistics, ensuring the availability of the items ordered and keeping up the delivery time, the various stages must be well planned. Also, at every stage, the time scheduled must be maintained and then only the items will reach the end customer ON TIME. In these two businesses lot of software tool is deployed besides many last-mile delivery vehicles. Unless all the parameters spelt by Valluvar are implemented in their true letter and spirit, it is impossible to achieve success in this NOVEL (அருவினை) business.

Not only for these two businesses but also for other businesses these points are valid.

Manage tools, time and methods - Handle even rare tasks!

3.2 Couplet: 687 / Chapter: 69
Emissary (தூது)

கடனறிந்து காலம் கருதி இடனறிந்து
எண்ணி உரைப்பான் தலை.

***A good leader assigns after understanding the job,
time factor and evaluating the location.***

Son: Dad, I think Valluvar advises a supervisor in this couplet rather than a manager. Am I right?

Father: Yes. He says a supervisor must understand the implications of the job fully before assigning the job to his subordinate. Otherwise, many shortcomings will be there and the chances of the job failing during execution are more.

Son: Dad, what do you mean by understanding a job? Typically in an engineering industry, what are the parameters to be understood by a supervisor before assigning a job?

Father: It depends on the nature of the job. Still, let me list a few parameters generally applicable to all the jobs.

- Job definition and the final target to be achieved.

- The step-by-step procedure to be adopted.

- The quality parameters to be adhered.

- Inspection and validation procedures at every stage.

- The time frame to complete the job.

- Manpower required to complete the job on time.

- Any software or special tool to be used.

- etc.

Not only understanding the above points, he must also decide whether everything will be done 'in house' or part of it can be outsourced (இடனறிந்து). Today, many companies outsource their jobs so that others' expertise can be utilized instead of adding resources to the company, increasing the overhead.

In Valluvar's days, there were not many industries. Still, he has written a couplet using such words which are more relevant for today's business.

Son: Dad, I require some practical examples to understand the couplet properly.

Father: I can quote today's **tender** business as an example. Any tender is a document that is meant for getting certain jobs done or for buying certain items required by a company. Most of the government departments follow tendering method for their procurement. In these tenders, the first and foremost point is the specification of the job to be carried out or the product to be supplied. The supplier must understand the tender specifications thoroughly (கடனறிந்து) and comply with every point mentioned in the tender. If the supplier misses out on even a small point in the specification or deviates from the specification, the tender will be rejected.

Similarly, any tender must be submitted **on time**. Otherwise, the Tender will be rejected. Also, the various time schedules given for supply, erection, commissioning etc. to be adhered to meticulously. This proves that Valluvar was right in mentioning 'time' as a critical parameter in this couplet.

Similarly, in a tender business the supplies may have to be made to different locations and the installations may have to be done in those locations. The term 'location' used by Valluvar has become a relevant one here. The tenderer has to consider all these points while preparing the tender so that wrong quotes may be avoided.

Understand fully and then assign!

3.3   Couplet: 770 / Chapter: 77
Glory of Army (படை மாட்சி)

நிலைமக்கள் சால உடைத்தெனினும் தானை
தலைமக்கள் இல்வழி இல்.

***Even though the army has longstanding soldiers
if there is no leader no way forward.***

Son: Dad, when there is no leader, can't the senior people jointly take things forward?

Father: If you see superficially, the answer will be yes. When you want the best team performance as required in a war front, then, a leader is definitely required.

Son: You mean to say even the senior most subordinate cannot manage?

Father: The head of a team requires a lot of leadership qualities apart from job knowledge. The senior most subordinate may have better job knowledge; but he will lack leadership qualities, particularly in handling emergencies. Let me tell you a modern management principle.

"Promoting the senior-most technician as a supervisor; Loss of a good technician and gain of a poor supervisor"

Son: Dad, do you mean to say in an organisation senior employees should not be promoted?

Father: No. You can promote them. But you have to give sufficient training in the supervisory role, particularly in leadership qualities of handling critical situations and taking decisions. Then only they can manage a team.

Sometimes the management may allow the senior employees together to handle the department without assigning the leadership role to any particular individual. This will have adverse effects. Every senior employee may take different decisions for a particular situation. This will create confusion and eventually, the work will suffer.

Here I want to mention yet another important management principle.

"One man cannot serve under two masters"

If this principle is violated the following situation will arise.

One worker commented.

'Mr. A' wanted me to paint green. 'Mr. B' wanted me to paint yellow. I painted Blue"

Therefore it is very important for an organization that a single individual leads the team even though the team has many experienced employees.

No leader – No progress!

3.4   Couplet: 634 / Chapter: 64
Ministry (அமைச்சு)

தெரிதலும் தேர்ந்து செயலும் ஒருதலையாச்
சொல்லலும் வல்லது அமைச்சு.

A competent manager is the one who understands (the job), chooses the right method and communicates head on.

Son: Dad, in this couplet Valluvar tries to define the competency of a manager. Is that right?

Father: Yes. Sometimes, the managers hesitate to communicate their opinion to their bosses, fearing the reason of 'what happens if it fails'. Keeping this in mind Valluvar insists that the managers must be confident of the subject before communicating. They must thoroughly understand the subject, the possible solutions and also the best way of implementing such solutions. This means the manager must have a holistic solution for any problem before going to his boss. If this is ensured, he need not fear about the possible failures and can communicate with courage without any hesitation. To emphasize this point Valluvar has used the word "ஒரு தலையாய்" meaning **"Head on Communications"**. This kind of communication can be achieved by written communication instead of oral communication. This is more pertinent in the case of major decisions of the management.

Son: Very interesting and highly practical dad. This means Valluvar expects the managers to be very competent in their jobs.

Father: Yes son. The managers (like ministers of those days) occupy the second line in the management hierarchy of an organisation.

They are closer to the lower-level employees of the organisation compared to the CEO and must take decisions holistically. Considering this aspect, Valluvar expects the managers to be very competent, knowledgeable and courageous. An organisation that has more such competent managers will be successful in its business.

Evaluate, decide and firmly communicate!

———— ·•· ————

3.5 Couplet: 468 / Chapter: 47
Knowledgeable Execution (தெரிந்து செயல்வகை)

ஆற்றின் வருந்தா வருத்தம் பலர்நின்று
போற்றினும் பொத்துப் படும்.

**A project started without a strategy will fail
even if more hands are deployed.**

Son: Is there anyone who will start a job without an idea?

Father: Yes, There are many. They know what they want, but they will start without proper planning. That is why today, the big companies while starting a project conduct many meetings and discuss every step of implementing the project. This is planned to micro-level boiling down to hours and minutes. The decisions are taken about who will do what, where and when etc. These procedures, once finalised will be documented and signed by the stakeholders. Any process is implemented as a teamwork. The documented process seldom fails, because it has a lot of **'failsafe'** precautions built into it to face any unforeseen eventuality. The 'failsafe' precautions are taken by the lateral thinking of the participants in a meeting.

Son: Dad, why Valluvar speaks about deploying too many hands?

Father: He has written this couplet for a king who plans to fight a war. Without any strategy, if a king thinks he can win a war just because he has more soldiers to fight, according to Valluvar, he will lose. In today's business also, if someone starts a project just because he has more finance, without any strategy or idea, naturally the project will fail. Many times I have observed that **'affulence by-passes strategy'**. One must be careful about this. Affluence can be anything like possessing excess funds, having competent manpower or having robust infrastructure. Deploying these without a defined process or strategy will eventually lead to failure.

Son: How to ensure the entire process beforehand?

Father: Process is a sequence of operations to be carried out to complete a project. Any project must be broken down into tasks and every task must be broken down into activities. The method of completing every activity has to be decided considering the tools required, the machinery to be deployed, the software to be used, the quality to be complied with and the time within which every activity has to be completed. The method of integrating all these things and creating a document of the project is called the definition of a process.

Numbers deployed do not matter; the strategy matters!

3.6 Couplet: 637 / Chapter: 64
Ministry (அமைச்சு)

செயற்கை அறிந்தக் கடைத்தும் உலகத்து
இயற்கை அறிந்து செயல்.

Even though one knows all the rules and regulations, he must be practical while performing.

Son: Dad! Valluvar has already said everyone must follow the documented procedure. But in this couplet he advises to be practical while performing a task. This is contradicting.

Father: It is not like that. Even though there are rules, regulations, SOPs etc., there may be eventualities for which the existing rules may not give a solution. This is more applicable while handling certain emergency and unforeseen situations and situations involving human factors. Under these circumstances, Valluvar says, one must take decisions considering the practical situation. Though many examples can be given in support of this statement, I will share a few here.

- **Emergencies:** In situations like medical emergencies, natural disasters, or accidents, practicality and quick decisions will be the immediate requirement rather than following the rules and regulations. If a worker swoons on the shop floor, instead of waiting for approval from the boss, moving the victim to the hospital will be the right example here.

- **Unforeseen circumstances:** When unexpected situations arise, a practical approach can help to find solutions that might not be covered by rules or regulations. A driver is supposed to follow the rules like driving on the left side, not overtaking on curves etc. But when some vehicle comes in front of him violating the rules, then, the driver must be practical rather than following the rules.

- **Creativity:** Following established rules may hinder free thinking. Practical thinking can lead to innovative solutions. Innovation is beyond rule books.

- **Humanitarian considerations:** In situations where following the rule book would lead to unfair or unjust outcomes, a practical approach allows empathy to take decisions. When an employee faces a personal problem, which requires a human approach, the rule book may not help.

- **Gray areas:** When rules are unclear and ambiguous, common sense and deviating from rules alone will help.

If a practical approach is not allowed the company may fail to tackle certain serious situations and the results may be irreparable. Today, there is a provision called **'Deviation Approval'** followed in organizations for ratifying such actions taken overlooking the rule book.

Be practical on critical situations!

3.7 Couplet: 691 / Chapter: 70
Getting along with the king (மன்னரைச் சேர்ந்தொழுகல்)

அகலாது அணுகாது தீக்காய்வார் போல்க
இகல்வேந்தர்ச் சேர்ந்தொழுகு வார்.

***Move with the king like one who neither goes closer
nor moves away from fire while warming.***

Son: I do not need any explanation for this couplet. Easy to understand.

Father: Yes. While moving with the top boss in an organisation one should be very cautious. He should always maintain a reasonable distance. This is the advice Valluvar gives to the managers.

In today's situation, I will say this concept is more applicable to the CEOs, because, the CEOs have to move very close to their subordinates to give a feeling that they treat them at par and at the same time they must be cautious to not to give too much of room to them. The reason being, under democratic situations, the CEO cannot keep his head high like a king. He must treat his subordinates at an equal level giving them respect as human beings and at the same time he must leave a feeling to the subordinates that they cannot put their hands on his shoulders. This is a special character that every CEO must develop to be successful in his role.

Son: Dad, I think the example of 'fire warming' given by Valluvar is really a good one.

Father: Yes son. Valluvar always uses apt examples in his couplets to make us remember the subject with ease.

Always maintain a distance from the boss!

Summing up the messages given above,

- Every department must have a leader.

- The leader must understand the full process of the task.

- The leader must plan the job in detail before assigning.

- The leader must have the courage to communicate with the boss.

- Importance of being practical.

- Subtle relationship of a boss and subordinate.

Awesome advices to the managers!

4

VALLUVAR
ON
HR-MANAGEMENT

4.0. The role of **HR** in an organisation

Son: Dad! How important is the HR department in an organisation?

Father: Today, in any business or industry there are many departments to carry out the various functions of the organisation. Every department is important for the organisation. Only when all the departments function successfully the organisation will be successful. The department will be successful only when it is managed by a competent team of employees with relevant experience. It is also equally important that every employee in a department performs well with utmost productivity. If a department has 'less competent' employees, then, the department will lag behind in its operations. This will affect not only the particular department but also the other departments, because, in business, every department is interdependent on the other. Therefore, the HR department which recruits, trains and inducts the employees for all the departments plays a vital role in the performance of the entire organisation. Besides recruiting the right candidates, the HR department is also responsible for maintaining the motivation of the employees during their employment in the organisation. The HR department ensures the happiness of the employees through many initiatives like,

- Compliance with statutory benefits of employees like ESI, PF, Bonus, etc.

- Support for children's education

- Medical insurance including the family

- Skill development and training

- Providing uniforms and shoes

- Awards and gifts on important occasions

- Transport facilities from home to office

- Fabulous perks

- Incentives

- Holiday packages etc.

In addition, in some organisations, the HR department goes to the extent of involving the family members in motivational schemes which emotionally attach them to the company and its welfare.

All these efforts lead to less employee attrition and ensure **'Total Employee Involvement'** in the organisation. I will say HR is the backbone of today's business or industrial establishments.

Son: Very interesting dad. Do you mean to say Valluvar has understood all these points while writing the Thirukkural?

Father: You will realize this after reading the couplets given below.

4.1 Couplet: 633 / Chapter: 64
Ministry (அமைச்சு)

பிரித்தலும் பேணிக் கொளலும் பிரிந்தார்ப்
பொருத்தலும் வல்லது அமைச்சு.

***A good management is one which takes out,
takes care, takes back and fits well.***

Son: Dad, what is this couplet? Confusing?

Father: Yes. It looks to be confusing. If you apply your mind properly you will understand an important HR point in this couplet. Now for your easy understanding, I am rewriting this couplet as below.

"A good management is one which takes out (from the competition), takes care (of the existing) and takes back (the resigned) and fits well (in the right position)"

Is it clear now?

Son: Yes Dad! Very interesting. I understand that Valluvar talks about having competent manpower in the organisation. Still, can you elaborate on this?

Father: In this couplet, Valluvar defines the competency of a good minister in a kingdom. He says a competent minister will pull out the capable functionaries from the enemy country and also he expects him not to lose his own talented functionaries by suitably taking care of them. Valluvar goes on to add that a competent minister will take back those who left his kingdom, adding on a special condition that these employees must be taken back in a fitting manner. A great advice to the ministers and highly relevant for today's management as well. The essence of the couplet is to emphasize the importance of having the right manpower in an organisation.

An organisation's primary strength is its competent employees. Other competencies are only secondary. **A competent employee performs many times better than a normal employee.** Certain studies conducted by McKinsey and Harvard Business School revealed that the top performers in an organisation can be three to five times more productive than an average employee. For this reason, an organisation cannot afford to lose them.

This is the reason why today companies pay very high salaries and take the best employees from the competitors. You can see this in all sectors. In the automobile sector in which I am familiar, I could see a lot of senior employees jumping companies in a 'criss-cross' manner. The HR department of big organisations works hard to take the best employees from the competitor organisations. This proves that Valluvar was right even two thousand years back.

Having understood the requirement for the best talent, nowadays, every organisation spends heavily on retaining its best talents. They allocate a sizable amount of funds for this. The main objective of the HR department is to keep the employees happy and reduce attrition. For this, many special facilities are offered to the employees. Even in providing these facilities, there is competition among industries. Every industry wants to prove their welfare measures are unique and better than the competitors. The Tamil terminology 'பேணிக்கொளலும்' which Valluvar has used in this couplet carries the ultimate meaning of the employee welfare measures. In a competitive world, losing an employee and hunting for replacement is a **'Non-Value Adding Activity'**. Substantial time and money is required for this. Instead, it is better to retain the existing employees. Valluvar means exactly this point in this couplet.

Many times good employees resign and leave the organisation. After some time they realize that they have committed a mistake and want to return back. Normally, the organisations take this as a prestige issue and the resigned employees are not welcomed back. But Valluvar says to take them back. Not only he advises to take them back, but also he recommends to offer them a fitting position in the organization (பிரிந்தார் பொருத்தலும்).

In seven words Valluvar has emphatically communicated a very important point of management that 'the talented employees are the backbone of an organisation' and at any cost, their strength must be maintained in the organisation.

Son: Dad, this is an eye-opener for me. When I start my business I will keep this point in mind and give utmost priority to retain the right manpower.

Father: Yes son. You must do it. I will also give a piece of advice to you. More than money the employees expect to be 'respected'. Unmindful of the position they hold, they expect to be respected as human beings. This is the key to employee retention. You must ensure that all the managers and officers in the organisation follow this principle and treat their subordinates including the workmen with due respect.

Grab the competent manpower and retain them!

———•◆•———

4.2 Couplet: 517 / Chapter: 52
Knowledgeable Performance (தெரிந்து வினையாடல்)

இதனை இதனால் இவன்முடிக்கும் என்றாய்ந்து
அதனை அவன்கண் விடல்.

***Let the job be assigned to one after evaluating that he
will complete this job because of these reasons.***

Son: Dad, this is a straight forward couplet. I can understand easily.

Father: Yes. It is very easy to understand. In this couplet, Valluvar wants the right man to be deployed to carry out a job. But, from where you will get the right person unless he is available within the organisation? This means the right person must be made available in the organisation. In other words, the right candidates must be selected during the recruitment stage itself. Naturally, it leads to the recruitment function of the HR department. This is the inner meaning of this couplet. In every couplet we must look at the implied or leading meaning to understand exactly what Valluvar means.

Son: Dad, how to recruit the right candidates? Can you explain in detail?

Farther: Selecting the right candidate is a critical function. It involves many stages of evaluation and filtration.

Job Specification: The HR department may not have sufficient knowledge about every department's employee competency requirement. For this, the respective department will prepare a detailed Job Specification for every job vacancy it requires. The specifications will consist of the required qualifications, age, experience, field of speciality etc.

Sourcing the resumes: Based on the above specifications the HR department will source the prospective candidates through various means like newspaper advertisements, Naukuri, Linked In etc.

Screening of the applications: Multilevel screening of resumes will be done and suitable resumes will be shortlisted.

Interviews: Thus, the shortlisted candidates will be called for personal interview by the HR department. Nowadays a Zoom interview is done initially followed by a personal interview. Conducting interviews is not an easy task. Within the short time frame of 30 to 45 minutes, the candidate's suitability has to be assessed. Normally I do not recommend a single person interviewing a candidate. It must be done by more than one and preferably three.

Pre-appointment checking: Before issuing the appointment order, it is advisable to take a feedback from the previous employer. The candidate's political affiliation or legal entanglement if any will be checked. The health of the employee is very important for his effective functioning and will be checked.

Issue of appointment offer: The employment must be offered with a higher salary than what he was getting earlier. Wherever applicable, employment bond and NDA clauses must be specified.

All the above efforts are only to select the right candidate. If this is done naturally Valluvar's statement of assigning the job for the right candidate is possible.

Right recruitment leads to the right man for the right job!

4.3   Couplet: 515 / Chapter: 52
Knowledgeable Performance (தெரிந்து வினையாடல்)

அறிந்தாற்றிச் செய்கிற்பாற்கு அல்லால் வினைதான்
சிறந்தானென்று ஏவற்பாற் றன்று.

Don't depute the one who doesn't know the ways and means
of performing a job, Just because he is aware of the job.

Son: Dad, This couplet is confusing me.

Father: Yes son. Superficially it is a little confusing. How come a person who knows his job, should not be deployed to carry out the job? Now we have to see the hidden meaning in this couplet. This couplet is applicable on two occasions.

Whenever fresh candidates are recruited from the colleges, the candidates with the best marks will be selected. This means the candidate will be very good in his subjects. Just because he has got a distinction, is it possible to deploy him on the job straight away? No; because he does not know the correct procedure of performing the job in the organisation. He has to be given training about the ways and means of carrying out his job including the step-by-step methods, the tools and machinery to be used, the quality to be maintained, the safety precautions to be taken etc. If such training is not given, whatever may be his distinction in the college, he cannot successfully carry out the job. This is what Valluvar means in this couplet.

The other situation is when an organisation recruits experienced candidates from other organisations. In this case also, though the candidate is experienced, he may not know the procedures followed in the new organisation. He may not know the operation of the specific machinery used here. He may not know the systems followed in executing the jobs in this new company. Therefore he must also be trained properly before putting him on the job.

In either case, a person cannot be deputed to carry out a job unless he is given **'on-the-job training'**. If this is not followed, he may commit mistakes and the mistakes may incur a loss to the organisation or sometimes it may lead to an accident also. The condition put forth by Valluvar by the terminology 'அறிந்தாற்றிச் செய்கிற்பாற்கு அல்லால்' clearly tells that unless one understands the ways and means of doing the job he should not be deployed to carry out the job. The remedy is offering proper 'on-the-job training'.

Training first - Job next!

———◆———

4.4 Couplet: 528 / Chapter: 53
Embracing the kith and kin (சுற்றம் தழால்)

பொதுநோக்கான் வேந்தன் வரிசையா நோக்கின்
அதுநோக்கி வாழ்வார் பலர்.

A king, instead of treating everyone at par, treats serially on merits, many will strive to be meritorious.

Son: To whom this couplet is applicable? To the functionaries (employees) of the kingdom or the citizens?

Father: Good question son. Though it is applicable for both, I will say this is more relevant for the functionaries in the kingdom. If the functionaries are motivated, they will take care of the citizens.

Son: Dad, how it is relevant to today's management?

Father: As Valluvar has mentioned earlier, the motivation of employees is very important to an organisation's success. There are many ways of inculcating motivation among employees. Recognizing and rewarding the better performers is the key to motivate the other employees. Though, a better working environment and better salaries are also motivating factors, as Valluvar has mentioned, ranking the employees through a fitting **Performance Appraisal System** will create internal competition among them. A performance 'benchmark' will be set by the top-ranking performer which will make other employees work hard to achieve the benchmark or even to surpass the benchmark. This is the essence of this couplet.

Son: Dad, how to implement performance appraisal in an organisation?

Father: Every organisation can define its own performance parameters and assign scores for each parameter, giving weightage based on its contribution towards productivity. Normally the employees will be assessed on two different categories.

1. **Values, Skills and Traits (Personal Character):** Responsibility, discipline, dress code, not absenting, not taking frequent leave, interpersonal relationship, obedience, duty consciousness, raising to occasions, compliance of SOP of the company and participation in the developmental activities like ISO, TQM, 5S etc.

2. **Productivity, Cost, Time and Quality Consciousness (Job Output):** Production output, Technical or job knowledge, Quality compliance, timely production, value engineering, cost saving, process improvement etc.

The employees will be evaluated on the parameters specified above and will be assigned marks. According to the rank, they will be awarded annual increments. The scores will be intimated to even to other employees so that anyone who got lesser marks in any of these parameters will try to improve on his performance which makes everyone to work towards improvement.

I can share my experience with you. You know very well that our company is exporting products to more than seventy countries and this was possible only because of the utmost quality we maintain in the products. For this, we follow all kinds of quality systems at every stage of production with stringent norms. Despite such stringent quality systems, there are some areas where the employee who carries out the job has to apply his mind and ensure perfection in quality. At a particular point in time, despite our stringent quality measures, the products we dispatched faced certain quality issues at the customer places. This came as a shock to us and we immediately convened a high-level meeting and analyzed the root cause. We found that most of the problems were minor in nature affecting the finish and appearance of the end product and caused by human errors. We deliberated and decided that only when the employees apply their minds on the job, such problems could be eliminated and no known quality system could resolve this. We announced a scheme of a cash award for the employees who find a fault or defect in the product before dispatch. This scheme worked well. Every employee started looking for any kind of defect in the product and started reporting to the management. The management took immediate action to address the situation and bring a system-based permanent solution. The employees responsible for committing such mistakes also changed their attitude and became cautious to avoid such faults. This action not only eliminated such defects but also improved the employee involvement in their work. Total employee involvement (TEI) is very important for the success of any organisation and such competition among the employees paves path for achieving this.

Son: Great dad! The fact that Valluvar could think two thousand years ahead on such subjects of employee involvement is really surprising. Good learning for me.

Internal competition – Enhanced performance!

4.5 Couplet: 518 / Chapter: 52
Knowledgeable performance (தெரிந்து வினையாடல்)

வினைக்குரிமை நாடிய பின்றை அவனை
அதற்குரிய னாகச் செயல்.

When a person is assigned a position, make him responsible for that position.

Son: Dad, what does Valluvar mean here?

Father: Valluvar touches upon another management principle of **'Responsibility Fixation'**. In many organisations, I find Responsibility Deviation instead of Responsibility Fixation.

A typical example will be, when a job is assigned to an individual, another person will also be made responsible for the same job. Here a responsibility clash occurs and confusion is created in decision-making. This situation must be avoided. Sometimes a job will be assigned to a group without mentioning the leader of the group. Here also the same situation will prevail.

Another situation will be when a superior officer assigns a job to his subordinate and continuously giving instructions to him on how to carry out the job. This is also bad. The subordinate must be given a free hand to carry out the task, with clear instructions to refer back to the superior when he gets a doubt. Or, the superior can monitor at regular intervals to ensure smooth going.

Son: Dad, is it not good if more brains are deployed in an activity? Why such water water-tight compartment must be there?

Father: No. Taking decisions can be done jointly by a team of people. But, the execution must be by a single person. A good leader always uses the brains of his subordinates by involving them in making decisions, but the ultimate execution must be by the leader only. Otherwise, if the project becomes a failure everyone will show hands on the other and the management cannot question anybody. If the project becomes a success, then everyone will claim that he is responsible for the success. Besides, when many people are made responsible for a job, the 'job involvement' may not be there by all participants and eventually the project may face issues. Visualizing these reasons, Valluvar wants to make the one who is assigned the job to be made responsible for executing the job. This is, in fact, the principle of today's management also.

Multiple responsibilities harm the job!

4.6 Couplet: 698 / Chapter: 70
Getting along with the king (மன்னரைச் சேர்ந்தொழுகல்)

இளையர் இனமுறையர் என்றிகழார் நின்ற
ஒளியோடு ஒழுகப் படும்.

One should be respected for his position rather than scorning him for being young or belonging to a particular race.

Son: Dad, I think this is an important couplet for me, because, I am young.

Father: Yes. Conventionally, everyone expects a certain age for a particular position in an organisation. If a young person is appointed in that position, the existing senior employees normally do not cherish it. Mostly they ill-treat him or insult him. Apparently, these things had happened in Valluvar's days also. For those seniors who indulge in such ill-treatment, Valluvar advises not to disrespect him just because he is young. He also advises that the youngster must be respected according to the position he holds. Valluvar uses a nice word in Tamil "ஒளியோடு ஒழுகப்படும்" which means one should be respected for the power he holds.

Son: Dad, Why Valluvar has used the word "racial" (இனமுறையர்) in this couplet?

Father: This is also happening. In an organisation where multinationals are employed this couplet is relevant. In the Gulf where I was working in the 1980s, many nationalities like Americans, French, English, Filipinos, Arabs, Africans and Indians were working. Some intelligent Asians or Africans used to occupy senior-level positions in the organisation. I have witnessed that some western country managers felt very embarrassed to work under them. This situation is similar to a black man occupying a higher position in the US. India is also in no way different. There are many caste discriminations still prevailing in India and it is manifesting in the organisations also. Therefore the situation is universal and Valluvar always gives universal solutions. He categorically says to respect the position one holds unmindful of age or race.

The word இனமுறையர் also refers to the relatives of the top management occupying higher positions. In this case also, Valluvar advises to 'respect the role' and ignore the other aspects.

Organisation is more important than personal considerations!

4.7 Couplet 514 / Chapter: 52
Knowledgeable performance (தெரிந்து வினையாடல்)

எனைவகையான் தேறியக்கண்ணும் வினைவகையான்
வேறாகும் மாந்தர் பலர்.

Irrespective of the tough selection process, everyone got selected will execute the same job differently.

Son: Dad, naturally everyone will work in his own way. What is the need for this couplet?

Father: If everyone carries out a job in his own way in an organisation, it may lead to many issues and waste of time. For example, if you ask three different persons to bring coffee to drink, one person may bring the coffee with milk and sugar mixed together, the next person may bring them separately and the third person may bring the coffee and milk pre-mixed and the sugar separately. Now, everyone has brought the coffee, but, in his own way. This cannot be accepted in an organisation because, in an organisation, a particular job must be done in a particular way only.

Let us assume that for a particular job vacancy, many candidates are required. To fill these vacancies, the interview was conducted very strictly and the required numbers of candidates have been selected. Valluvar says, despite the serious selection process (எனைவகையான் தேறியக் கண்ணும்) the selected candidates if allowed to carry out the job, everyone will carry out the job in his own way. This will lead to the usage of different tools, following different methods and may end up taking different times. For this reason, this couplet implies that, for every job, the method of performing the job must be defined. Everyone who is assigned that particular job must be **trained** in the same procedure. In other words, the procedures must be standardized. Such standardization reduces conflicts, eliminates the usage of different tools by different individuals and saves time. If the job contains a set of activities, which are performed repeatedly in an organisation, then, a **Standard Operating Procedure (SOP)** has to be created. For example, 'purchase' is a job involving many activities like getting quotations, applying taxes, arranging transportation, making payments etc. For such jobs, SOP is a must. Otherwise, everyone will buy materials in his own way leading to confusion and loss.

Therefore, the terminology 'வினைவகையான் வேறாகும் மாந்தர் பலர்' used in this couplet bearing the meaning that "even if the best of the candidates were selected everyone will perform in his own way", signifies the importance of standardization of the process.

Standardization ensures easy compliance!

4.8 Couplet: 562 / Chapter: 57
Rule without scaring (வெரு வந்த செய்யாமை)

கடிதோச்சி மெல்ல எறிக நெடிதாக்கம்
நீங்காமை வேண்டு பவர்.

Pretend big and punish less, if the benefit of one's long service is not to be parted with.

Son: Dad, What does Valluvar mean in this couplet?

Father: Valluvar emphasizes the importance of long service by an employee in an organisation. In employment, nothing can replace the experience of an employee. To insist on this point Valluvar brings in an example where an employee having long experience commits a mistake which cannot be ignored without a punishment. When such an event happens Valluvar advises the management to impose less punishment on him, because, his long experience is important to the organisation. While giving this advice, he also gives a tactical suggestion that the management must give an impression to the employee that the mistake committed by him is too big and deserves severe punishment and despite that he is being punished less.

Son: Dad, why Valluvar wants him to be punished less?

Father: There is a reason. If the employee is punished heavily, he might leave the organisation. But, Valluvar does not want to lose experienced employees at any cost, because it is difficult to get such experienced hands from outside. Even if the employee does not leave the job, he may continue to work with demotivation. Then again, his full output may not be available to the organisation. Valluvar considers the organisation's interest to be more important and he does not want the organisation to suffer in any manner. For this reason, he makes such a unique piece of advice which is not heard of today. I too feel Valluvar's advice is correct.

Son: Dad, Why Valluvar wants the management to pretend as though the mistake committed is a big one? It doesn't sound professional to me.

Father: Here again Valluvar keeps the organisation's interest at the forefront. He wants the employee to get a feeling that the organisation has done a big favour by not giving him a big punishment that he deserved. This will create a feeling of indebtedness within the employee and he will try to perform better and compensate by involving more in his job.

Son: Great indeed. Valluvar applies his mind from the organisation point of view and offers such suggestions. He does not want the employee's motivation to be hurt at any cost.

Father: But, the same Valluvar has told in couplet No.550, if the mistake committed by an employee is intentional and detrimental to the organisation, then, he must be removed from the organisation without any hesitation. This means this particular couplet is applicable for mistakes that are not intentional and detrimental to the organisation. This advice is very knowledgeable and can emanate only out of rich experience. It looks Valluvar had such experiences too in his period.

Never leave an experienced employee!

4.9 Couplet: 550 / Chapter: 55
Justice (செங்கோன்மை)

கொலையிற் கொடியாரை வேந்தொறுத்தல் பைங்கூழ்
களைகட் டதனொடு நேர்.

***A king eliminating the terrorists is as good as a farmer
removing the weeds to safeguard the crops.***

Son: Dad, Valluvar seems to be very tough in this couplet.

Father: Yes son. He is tough. He doesn't want any terrorist to be in
a kingdom in the interest of the country. The corollary is also true.
In today's organisations, there are some employees who indulge
in anti-organisational activities. This is equivalent to terrorism in
a country. These bad elements are very dangerous and will create
problems to the organisation by instigating other employees.
Besides, they may also indulge in sabotaging the machinery,
equipment etc. In India kind of democratic countries politics may
enter into the employee unions and create still worse problems that
will paralyze the organisation. Many 'lockouts' have taken place
because of this kind of interference. According to Valluvar, such
employees who are dangerous to the organisation are like terrorists
in a country and to be weeded out to safeguard the organisation.

Son: Dad, do you have any experience of such situations?

Father: Yes son. I do have. Once, some of my company employees
were instigated by outsiders and started indulging in such
anti-company activities. Normally I love my employees and I did not
want to punish anyone. But this problem started aggravating every
day and within three years became intolerable. Then I took a strong

decision and suspended the problematic employees and adhering to the labour rules terminated the key troublemakers. Since then, the employees have been thinking that the management is weak and will not take any drastic action. But, the severe action taken by me changed their impression and yielded results and the other troublesome employees became polite and the problem was solved. Good employees supported this act of the management. At that point of time, I have not read "Thirukkural". But his principle was adopted by me to solve the problem and it worked. Thiruvalluvar teaches justice, besides discipline. Let us decode and get benefited.

Never tolerate terrorism and betrayal!

Summing up the messages given above,

- Recruit the right candidates.

- Retain the existing employees.

- Importance of 'on the job' training.

- Encouraging the employees based on performance.

- Respecting the role and responsibility.

- Importance of Systems and SOP.

- Proper punishment and elimination of troublesome employees.

- And much more.

***A prophet's advice on unique HR principles
for today's business!***

5

VALLUVAR
ON
MARKETING MANAGEMENT

5.0. Marketing

Son: Dad, how come Valluvar has written couplets on Marketing Management?

Father: Not directly. The advices given by him to a king for tackling the neighbouring kings applies to today's competition management. In those days when kings were ruling, they had to keep the neighbouring kings in good relations to avoid war. For this, the king sends his emissaries regularly to meet the other kings, to maintain a cordial relationship. If the emissary is not a competent person, then, he spoils the relationship. Having understood the role of an emissary, Valluvar has defined the qualities required for an emissary in the Chapter 'தூது' which means emissary. Despite his efforts for a good relationship, the neighbouring king may plan to wage a war against the king. Then, the espionage becomes important and the king deploys spies for espionage. Valluvar defines how a spy must function in the chapter 'ஒற்று' meaning **espionage**. Once the spy tells the king that war is imminent, then, the king has to prepare himself for the war. Valluvar also advises on war **preparations** by a king.

All the above three aspects of emissary, espionage and war preparations narrated by Valluvar are very much applicable to today's marketing management and are being practiced. Let us see the similarity of roles.

1. **Emissary:** Salesperson who meets the customers.

2. **Espionage:** Market Intelligence and market survey.

3. **War Strategy:** Product launch and sales promotion.

The success of a company lies in the successful marketing of its products. Even if an organisation has certain unique technology, the best quality and the best features, if it fails in marketing, all these competencies will be in vain. To succeed in the market, the company must adopt and implement various market development initiatives. Otherwise, failure is inevitable. Valluvar has clearly conveyed this message through many of his couplets. All the ideas expressed by Valluvar about the preparations to be made by a king before going to a war are equally applicable to companies entering into today's business competition. Let's take a closer look at Valluvar's ideas on "Marketing Management"

5.1   Couplet: 465 / Chapter: 47
Knowledgeable execution (தெரிந்து செயல்வகை)

வகையறச் சூழாது எழுதல் பகைவரைப்
பாத்திப் படுப்பதோர் ஆறு.

***Waging a war without a strategy will channelize
the entry of the enemy.***

Son: Dad, Valluvar talks about the importance of 'strategy' in this couplet. Am I right?

Father: Yes. This couplet emphasizes the importance of evolving a strategy by a king before waging a war. If there is any flaw in the strategy, the enemy will exploit the situation and infiltrate into the king's army. This idea is equally applicable to today's business, especially when **launching a new product**. That's why 'New Product

Launch' is considered to be a very serious affair by the business world and handled as a major marketing initiative. Product Launch is planned for months, in terms of displaying the product features and strengths, counteracting all the strengths of the competitors, attracting customers by advertisements, TV appearances, positioning at the right time and above all launching at the right price. If there is any flaw in any of these plans, the 'product launch' will fail. Launch failure is considered to be a serious failure in the business circle and it takes a long time to recover from it. That's why Valluvar says never launch without holistic planning and strategy through his words "வகையறச் சூழாது எழுதல்" in Tamil. If there is any flaw in launching a product, today's competitors will keenly watch it (like the enemy of a nation) and easily exploit the situation by magnifying these flaws and spreading them to customers. This is meant by the words"பகைவரைப் பாத்திப் படுப்பதோர் ஆறு". Therefore, while launching a new product, one must take utmost care in the planning to reach the customers successfully.

Son: Dad, Can you give me some examples of Launch failures?

Father: Yes son. The following examples depict launch failures.

1. **Google Glass (2014):** The smart Glass failed during its launch because of its high price and customer doubt affecting privacy. The market study before launch was not done properly which resulted in the failure.

2. **Samsung Galaxy Note 7 (2016):** Rushed launch led to battery recall and eventual discontinuation.

3. **Bisleri** a brand known for bottled water failed in the launch of Bisleri POP sugar sodas in 2006 due to its confusion with Bisleri water.

4. **Onida TV** in India failed during the launch due to its wrong positioning in the market and wrong advertising strategies.

5. **Amazon Fire Phone (2014):** Poorly received due to limited app selection and high price.

Many more examples can be given to support Valluvar's point of implementing a product launch without preparation.

These examples illustrate the importance of careful planning, market research and testing before launching a product or service. Factors like pricing, marketing, and user experience can make or break a launch.

Well-planned product launch - Goes well with the market!

5.2 Couplet: 750 / Chapter: 75
Bulwark (அரண்)

எனைமாட்சித் தாகியக் கண்ணும் வினைமாட்சி
இல்லார்கண் இல்லது அரண்.

Irrespective of having special protections, if an effective war strategy is lacking, the bulwark will fail.

Son: Dad, What kind of strategy is required for an army and how it is related to marketing?

Father: Let us assume that a kingdom is having a bulwark specially built with all protections. The army also has full of trained competent soldiers and lieutenants with all arms and ammunitions.

While facing a war, if an effective strategy is not planned and kept in place, all these competencies will become useless and even the strong bulwark will give way to the enemies.

In the case of a business, the marketing is also like a war. Every market requires a strategy. The company may have quality products with excellent features and also may have a highly experienced marketing team. If the marketing team does not have a proper marketing strategy, the company will fail and the competitor will penetrate into the market.

Son: What do you mean by Marketing Strategy in business?

Father: Strategy is a set of ideas to be enacted before entering a market. In today's marketing, though there are many aspects to be considered that are specific to the product and market, I will give you a general strategy which can be applied to all products. It is called 4Ps of marketing.

1. **Product**

2. **Price**

3. **Place**

4. **Promotion**

Product: This means the company must have the right product which the market needs. Also, it must have better features than the competitors and there must be more Unique Selling Propositions (USPs).

Price: This is very important. Pricing has to be carefully done considering the competition and the end customer's affordability. The pricing must match with the features, quality and the warranty offered. If a higher price compared to the competitors is fixed, then, it must be justifiable in the market. Sometimes volume discounts will help.

Place: This refers to the places where the products are sold, the distribution channel and the logistics made available. Distribution today has become a critical parameter when the cost of logistics and delivery time compared to a competitor has become a choice for the customer. Many customers do not want to wait for the supplies to arrive and this makes the 'order to delivery time' a critical parameter in marketing.

Promotion: The first and foremost point in marketing is communicating the USPs of our products to the buyers. This is called 'Sales Promotion'. Today there are a lot many ways of carrying out sales promotional activities. Let me brief you a few.

- Product Catalogues / Fliers
- PowerPoint Presentations / Product Videos
- Advertisements
- Road Shows / Exhibitions
- Digital Marketing Techniques
- Social Media Marketing etc.

The company must choose the relevant one(s) for the market and carry out these activities. Training the sales team in competing competitions is very important. Sales promotion is the most important of all the strategic points.

Son: Dad, Can you give me some examples of companies that became successful by following the 4Ps philosophy?

Father: There are many. I will give a few examples.

- **Apple:**

  Product: Innovative design-driven products like iPhones and Mac Books.

  Price: Premium pricing strategy to maintain brand image and quality perception.

  Place: Strategic distribution through Apple Stores, online platforms, and select retailers.

  Promotion: Effective advertising, Road Shows, and loyalty programs.

- **Coca-Cola:**

  Product: Iconic beverage brand with a consistent taste and quality.

  Price: Competitive pricing strategy to maintain market share.

  Place: Wide distribution network across various channels, including retail, restaurants, and vending machines.

  Promotion: Memorable advertisements, promotions, campaigns and sponsorships.

- **Nike:** (manufacturing sports shoes, shirts, bags, etc.)

  Product: High-quality, innovative athletic footwear and apparel.

  Price: Premium pricing strategy to maintain brand image and quality perception.

Place: Strategic distribution through Nike Stores, online platforms and select retailers.

Promotion: Effective advertising, sponsorships, and influencer partnerships.

These companies have successfully implemented the 4Ps to create effective marketing strategies, driving their growth and success. Unless these strategic decisions are effectively implemented the company cannot win the market. This is the implied meaning of this couplet.

Son: Can you give me an example of a good company failing due to poor marketing?

Father: A classic example of a good company failing due to poor marketing is the story of Segway. Segway was a revolutionary personal transportation device that was launched in 2001 with great fanfare. Despite its innovative technology and potential to transform the way people move around, Segway failed to gain widespread acceptance due to poor marketing strategies like unrealistic hype for the product, lack of clarity on end users, very high launch price etc.

Son: Dad, some more examples?

Father: Yes. Some Indian Companies

- **Nokia India** failed to adapt to changing market trends and consumer preferences, leading to a decline in sales and eventual exit from India.

- **HMT Watches** failed to revamp its brand image and product line, leading to a decline in sales and eventual closure.

- **Sahara Group** failed to diversify and rebrand, leading to financial struggles and regulatory issues.

- **Videocon** failed to compete with global brands, leading to financial struggles and the eventual sale of assets.

Son: Can you list the mistakes committed by these companies?

Father: The common mistakes committed were in marketing.

- Failure to adapt to changing market trends.

- Ineffective branding and positioning.

- Poor customer engagement.

- Lack of innovation.

- Inadequate market research.

Son: Thank you Dad for cautioning me with these failure examples.

Father: You have to thank Valluvar who has cautioned about strategy through this couplet.

Poor marketing pulls down all other competencies!

———•———

5.3 Couplet: 684 / Chapter: 69
Emissary (தூது)

அறிவுரு ஆராய்ந்த கல்வி இம்மூன்றன்
செறிவுடையான் செல்க வினைக்கு.

The one having good general knowledge, good personality and in-depth subject knowledge must go as an ambassador.

Son: Dad, whatever this couplet says is understandable for an ambassador. How do you connect this with today's marketing?

Father: Good question. The ambassador of a country very often meets the other country's king mainly to communicate the message from his king and get the objective of his mission successful. In other words, his job is to convince the other country's king with reasons supported by an analytical approach and make the other king accept his points. Today a marketing man's job is also to convince the customers by explaining the USPs (Unique Selling Propositions) of his products. Ultimately both do the same job of convincing the other party.

Son: Agreed Dad. What is the message in this couplet?

Father: Valluvar says, a person having vast general knowledge, excellent personality and 'in-depth' product knowledge, must go for marketing. Every word used by Valluvar in this couplet carries a fabulous meaning that qualifies a perfect marketing man. I will explain to you word by word.

Must have good general knowledge (அறி): Any marketing person, when he meets his customer will not start talking about his product straight away. To start with, he will talk about general subjects like recent happenings in society, sports, music or any subject which is of interest to the customer. This will form a strong base for further discussions. He will carefully avoid controversial subjects like politics, religion etc. A good marketing guy always enquires and finds out about the customer's favorite subjects before meeting him. A small praise about his achievements will make the customer happy and he will like to hear more from the marketing guy.

To accomplish the above, the marketing guy keeps himself updated on all the subjects happening around. He must have a habit of reading newspapers or social media to get to know the latest happenings. This will help him to start a smooth conversation with the customer.

Excellent Personality (உரு): We all know that a marketing guy must possess a good personality. Not necessary that he must be a handsome person. A good marketing guy enhances his personality with an appealing dress, well-shaven face or nicely trimmed beard and making himself a presentable guy. He also tunes his language with a pleasing tone in such a way that the person sitting in front of him will listen to what he says. Valluvar has used the word "உரு" which means 'personality' and has clearly avoided using the word "திரு" in Tamil which means 'handsome'.

In-depth product knowledge (ஆராய்ந்த கல்வி): In-depth product knowledge comes only when a research is done on the product being represented and also on the similar products available in the market. According to Valluvar, the marketing guy should have done research on his products to know the Unique Selling Proposition (USPs) and also the weakness of competitor products. A good marketing man does not abuse the competitors' products and avoids negative marketing and at the same time does not fail to cleverly communicate the deficiencies of the competitors' products with a smiling face. Communication in marketing is very important and it comes out only when the marketing guy possesses in-depth product knowledge.

Keeping the above requirements in mind, the HR department, while recruiting a marketing candidate, assesses his personality and verifies his general knowledge. After recruitment, they are imparted with intensive training on the products. Valluvar has understood the importance of a marketing person two thousand years ago and defined his qualities.

Depute the competent to conquer the market!

5.4   Couplet: 769 / Chapter: 77
Glory of army (படை மாட்சி)

சிறுமையும் செல்லாத் துனியும் வறுமையும்
இல்லாயின் வெல்லும் படை.

An army will win if it does not have soldiers lesser in numbers, hating their own king and poverty-stricken.

Son: Dad, it seems the message given for an army through this couplet applies to the marketing team in an organisation. Am I right?

Father: Yes. You are right. Valluvar says three important criteria for a marketing team.

1. **Less manpower:** The marketing team must have sufficient number of personnel to cover the marketing area. The marketing area may be a state, a country or even many countries. Every location must be covered and manned by a marketing person. If the company leaves certain locations vacant, the competitors will penetrate through that location and take our market share.

2. **Demotivated team:** The marketing team in an organisation should not have executives who have developed hatred feeling against their own organisation. In other words, the team should not consist of demotivated marketing executives or managers. This is an important point for the marketing team. If there are demotivated employees in production or other departments it may affect the productivity of the particular department only. But, if there are demotivated employees in marketing, it will affect the entire organisation's performance. When the marketing team goes to the field they will face the marketing guys from the competitors who normally praise and glorify their organisation to win the deal. If our marketing team is demotivated they cannot fittingly reply to the competition wholeheartedly and will lack the fire which a marketing team is supposed to possess to conquer the competition. Valluvar has clearly understood this point and concludes that a demotivated army can never win over an enemy and it is equally applicable to today's business too.

3. **Financially weak employees:** Another important criterion for a marketing team as per Valluvar is that the team should not consist of employees suffering from financial inadequacy in their personal life. If such a needy person goes for marketing, he may compromise on his dress code, travel mode and other 'self-portrayal' measures which are important for marketing. Due to these reasons, today companies take care of the marketing team with good salaries, perks, travel and stay allowances and above all fabulous performance incentives. Sometimes the

salaries of the marketing team are so high that the other departments envy them. Some companies while recruiting the marketing manpower check their social and financial background and ensure minimum adequacy.

Whatever Valluvar has said in this couplet is being practiced by big corporate companies today. Medium and small-scale companies can also follow these criteria to keep the marketing employees in good motivation and bring more business to the company.

No team motivation – No market!

5.5   Couplet: 682 / Chapter: 69
Emissary (தூது)

அன்பறிவு ஆராய்ந்த சொல்வன்மை தூதுரைப்பார்க்கு
இன்றி யமையாத மூன்று.

***The inevitable qualities of an emissary will be
kindness, knowledge and competent communication.***

Son: Dad, why a marketing guy should have kindness?

Father: Good question. The word kindness in this couplet means **'good human relations'**. The emissary who is deputed to other countries should have the capability of attracting the people around and establishing a good and lovable relationship. If this is established his job becomes easy to accomplish. In modern business also everyone will agree that the marketing guy who can establish a good relationship with the customers can win an order easily. Today's marketing is more of relationship marketing. That is why today's marketing guys carry some seasonal gifts to hand over to customers before starting the conversation. Even in those days, the emissaries used to carry special gifts from their country and present them to the other country's king before starting the dialogue. Here, Valluvar wants the marketing guy to maintain good human relations with everyone. Now I hope you understand.

Son: Yes Dad. It is clear now. Valluvar also wants the marketing guy to have good knowledge. What knowledge?

Father: As I told you already in another couplet, the marketing guy must have general knowledge and also product knowledge. The general knowledge is to set an amicable ground for discussions. The product knowledge is to convince the customer about the superiority of his product over the competitors' products. For this, he must learn about competitors' products also. A marketing guy must have strong knowledge of competitor products in terms of their quality, functionality and price. This will help in convincing a customer in his favour when competition is tough. Therefore the marketing man must be a knowledgeable person in all the above.

Son: The third point Valluvar makes is good communication. What does he mean by good communication?

Father: Good Communication is the most important quality of a marketing guy. Valluvar uses the terminology "ஆராய்ந்த சொல்வன்மை" meaning, ***"evaluated and competent communication skill"***. When he says evaluated, he means evaluating the equivalent products available in the market with respect to his own products. Competent communication skill means the way of explaining the product, the features and the USPs of his products to the customers. A good marketing guy does not criticize competitors' products openly, though he will bring out the deficiencies politely. Normally a good marketing guy will not spell out the price details of his product immediately upon starting the conversation. Prices are the last one to be communicated, that too, when the customer asks. Till such time he explains the features of his product and clarifies the doubts of the customer. Sometimes allowing the customer to raise more queries will be a good idea. Speaking tone, timing of communicating the critical points and being assertive about own products are certain factors of communication that make a difference.

Son: Dad, it is surprising to note that a poet not involved in governance talks of such interactions so vividly which when applied to today's situation, fits in as if told for today's marketing team.... Great!

Maintain marketing traits– Maneuver the market!

————•◉•————

5.6   Couplet: 685 / Chapter: 69
Emissary (தூது)

தொகச்சொல்லித் தூவாத நீக்கி நகச்சொல்லி
நன்றி பயப்பதாம் தூது.

A good emissary collates, explains, eliminates irrelevancies and communicates cheerfully to derive the benefit.

Son: Dad, here again, Valluvar guides a marketing guy on how to communicate effectively. Am I correct?

Father: Yes. According to Valluvar, effective communication is very important for business success and also in personal life. I have seen him giving thrust to communication in many of his couplets.

Son: What is special in this couplet?

Father: He says that whatever has to be communicated must be **compiled** nicely eliminating the irrelevant things. This is what is happening today. Every salesperson prepares a PPT presentation in which the subject to be communicated is compiled properly in seriatim. Some executives may, out of curiosity, add certain irrelevant things. Valluvar has predicted this and advises removing such irrelevant matters from the compilation. His idea is that the presentation must be direct and focused on the subject. The word 'தொகச் சொல்லி' used by Valluvar exactly depicts the PPT presentation of today. Besides the above, Valluvar advices the marketing guy to explain the compilation cheerfully with a smiling face (நகச் சொல்லி).

Next in order Valluvar uses the terminology "நன்றி பயப்பதாம்" meaning eventually benefitting his country (company). In today's marketing training courses, there is a teaching. A sales executive can spend any amount of time in presales gestures like greeting the customer, praising him for his achievements and also can spend more time praising his own company and his products glorifying them in a fitting manner. But, at the end of the conversation, he should not leave the room without asking a question to the customer. "Sir, when can I expect your orders?" This is what valluvar means in this couplet.

Correct Communication – Convinced Customer!

5.7   Couplet: 689 / Chapter: 69
Emissary (தூது)

விடுமாற்றம் வேந்தர்க்கு உரைப்பான் வடுமாற்றம்
வாய்சோரா வன்க ணவன்.

The right emissary never utters a faulty word even by mistake while communicating with the other king.

Son: Dad, How can an emissary use a faulty word?

Father: It happens. I categorize the faulty words in two aspects. One aspect is revealing certain secrets which are not supposed to be revealed to a customer. For example, his company's products might have faced a failure somewhere. This should never be revealed to a customer. The marketing guy may know certain IPR secrets of the product and such secrets should not be revealed to the customer. There may be internal problems within his organisation, which he should never reveal to his customers. Like this, any information that is detrimental to the business transaction should be avoided and even by mistake should not be communicated.

The other aspect is, uttering unparliamentary or impolite words during the conversation. A marketing guy, in general, will be a kind of socialising guy to maintain friendships. In such a lifestyle, he would have developed a habit of using certain impolite words like "bloody" "nonsense" etc. Valluvar says that a marketing guy should have the mental makeup to avoid such bad words during marketing conversations. Sometimes, the customer may provoke him by abusing his company and his products. Even under such situations the marketing guy should react very politely and should avoid bad words. Once he uses a bad word, his own organisation will not tolerate him, because, it will reflect on the image of the company and affect the business. Here I want to quote another couplet of Valluvar supporting this point.

இனிய உளவாக இன்னாத கூறல்
கனியிருப்பக் காய்கவர்ந் தற்று. *(குறள் - 100)*

Using bad words when good words are available is like eating raw vegetables when ripe fruits are available. (couplet - 100)

Valluvar believes in flawless communication. This is very much applicable to both business and life.

Bad words – Bad Marketing!

Summing up the messages given above,

- Qualities of a good marketing person.

- Importance of good human relations in marketing.

- Importance of communication in marketing.

- Advantage of a happy marketing team.

- No Strategy - No business.

- Importance of Product Launch.

Valluvar defines certain rules for marketing!

6

VALLUVAR'S ADVICE
TO
RESEARCH & DEVELOPMENT

6.0. The significance of R&D in an organisation.

Son: Dad, are you sure that Valluvar has given some ideas for Research and Development also?

Father: Sure. His ideas about R&D are fabulous. Research is not an easy field. It is a field managed by intellectuals. R&D is the art of bringing the unknown to the known. It requires intelligence, imagination, perseverance and a character to face challenges and defeats. R&D drives innovation and leads to new products, services, and processes. It enables companies to stay ahead of the competition. It improves the existing products, making them more efficient, cost-effective and customer-friendly. It enhances competitiveness. Organisations that invest in R&D are better positioned to adapt to changing market conditions and customer needs. R&D fosters partnerships with academia, industry peers and government entities leading to knowledge sharing and new opportunities. R&D supports long-term growth and investments made in R&D today will result in the profitability of the company in the future. R&D provides Insights into organisations to stay informed about emerging technologies, trends and customer preferences. Organisations with strong R&D departments are often perceived as industry leaders, enhancing their brand reputation.

For such an important department Valluvar has enacted certain guidelines through some of his couplets and let us see them now.

6.1   Couplet: 678 / Chapter: 68
Mode of execution (வினை செயல் வகை)

வினையான் வினையாக்கிக் கோடல் நனைகவுள்
யானையால் யானையாத் தற்று.

Completing a job along with another job, is like capturing an elephant using another elephant.

Son: Why should we carry out another job when one job is being carried out? Is it not better to do one at a time?

Father: This is to save a great amount of time. This phenomenon is called **Concurrent Engineering** in today's R&D.

Son: Dad, Can you explain to me about the 'Concurrent Engineering' in R&D?

Father: Before explaining Concurrent Engineering, I must explain to you the various steps followed by the R&D department to develop a new product. The example given here applies to a typical engineering product, though the chemical and other products will slightly vary depending on the nature of the product.

Market Input: The first step in R&D is to get the details of the product as required for the market. The Market Input will define the customer requirement, the utility of the product, the functioning of the product with the features required, the quality requirement and the competitors offering available in the market and above all the prevailing price details.

Concept Document: Based on the Market Input, the design department will create a concept document which is written in text form narrating the design details of the product. The concept document will contain the macro level Block Diagrams and Schematics of the proposed product. It will also have the standards to be complied with, approvals to be obtained and validation procedures to ensure the development of a quality product. This document will also define the cost required for developing the product (Project Cost) and will set a Target Price for the product being developed based on the market price.

Development of Detailed Drawings: The next step is to develop design drawings, schematics and circuit diagrams pertaining to the Mechanical, Electrical, and Electronic designs of the product. This includes the Software Flow diagrams as required.

Bill of Materials (BOM): Once the detailed drawings, sub-assembly drawings and final assembly drawings are ready, the detailed Bill of Materials of the proposed product will be arrived at. The cost for the total BOM will be calculated and the procurement of the parts and components can start now.

Prototype Development: Prototype is the first product to be assembled immediately upon getting all the components as per BOM. The prototype will be assembled conforming to the drawings made.

Testing and Validation: The Prototype developed will be thoroughly tested as defined in the concept document to ensure proper functioning of the product. At this stage, many revisions of the product will take place before passing the product for production.

Process and Product Engineering: Even though the Prototype is tested to be successful, the product will not be directly taken up for production. It will go through an engineering adaptation to make the product production worthy. This activity generates the required Production Procedure, Quality Parameters, Jigs and Fixtures required for production etc. This Engineering Department adds value to the product design to ensure seamless production.

Pilot Lot Production: The pilot lot is a sample lot production. Despite all the above precautions taken to productionise the product, the production department will not start producing the full capacity straight away. A minimum quantity will be decided as Pilot Lot Production to test the production line.

Final Production: Only when the Pilot Lot is produced successfully the product will be taken up for final production.

Son: Great dad. Now I can understand the importance of R&D. Where is Concurrent Engineering coming here?

Father: Concurrent Engineering is the action of involving other departments like Production, Engineering, Service etc., during the course of product development. The Engineering Department may have to make many moulds, Jigs, Fixtures etc., for production which will normally take a lot of time. If this activity starts after the development of the product by R&D, it will delay the product launch heavily. To reduce this delay, the development of these items will be started simultaneously along with the development of the product. This saves a lot of time. Similarly, the customer support department can prepare their service infrastructure, spare parts planning etc. simultaneously thus saving time. This kind of simultaneous development by other departments along the course of the design and development of the main product is called Concurrent Engineering. Because of this the **'Time to go**

to Market' is greatly reduced. This is what Valluvar exactly means in this Couplet using the words 'விளையான் விளையாக்கிக் கோடல்'. This principle can be applied for all processes, wherever possible. But it is more relevant for today's R&D and is being practiced.

Son: Dad, Valluvar again brings an elephant as an example here. How it is relevant here?

Father: Valluvar is referring to the traditional method of capturing wild elephants using a trained elephant, called 'Kumki' elephant. The trained elephant is used to lure and subdue the wild elephant, using its saliva (நனை கவுள்) which acts as a tranquilizer that relaxes and tames the wild elephant. This is the easiest way of capturing a wild elephant which otherwise is a tough task.

Completing a job along with another job is as easy as capturing an elephant using another elephant. Otherwise it will be a tough task. Very interesting example.

Completing jobs alongside – Complements time saving!

6.2. Couplet: 663 / Chapter: 67
Effective performance (வினைத் திட்பம்)

கடைக்கொட்கச் செய்தக்கது ஆண்மை இடைக்கொட்கின்
ஏற்றா விழுமம் தரும்.

A good management reveals (its' developments) at the end; revealing in-between yields negative results.

Son: Dad, I think Valluvar talks about IPR in this couplet. Am I right?

Father: Yes. Today every company is striving hard to capture a bigger market share. The companies have also understood that 'innovation' is the key for getting additional market share and sustaining it. For this, the company's R&D department is burning its midnight oil and trying to innovate new functions and features in its products. Many companies invest huge money in bringing a completely new product and the company wants to take the market by surprise using this new product or idea. Severe competition is going on now in this direction. When such confidential developments are being made, leaking any information about such developments in between (இடைக்கொட்கின்), will be detrimental to the organization (ஏற்றா விழுமம் தரும்).

Son: Any example of such a leakage of IPR ?

Father: Under severe competitive situations, many such IPR scandals have taken place. I am just furnishing a few which has come to my knowledge through media.

- **Coca-Cola's Secret Formula:** In the 1970s, a company employee attempted to sell the secret formula to its competitor, but he was caught. However, in 2006, a former employee stole a confidential document containing the formula and tried to sell it to the same competitor again. Although the theft was discovered, the incident highlighted the risks of internal leaks.

- **Procter & Gamble's (P&G)**: In 2001, a former P&G employee stole confidential data on new products and sold it to a competitor. P&G sued the competitor and the incident led to a significant loss of intellectual property.

- **DuPont's Kevlar Technology:** In the 1980s, a DuPont employee sold confidential information about its Kevlar production to a competitor, leading to a significant loss of market share and revenue.

Like this, there are many incidents of confidential information leaking. Valluvar has warned about it.

Son: There is no way of preventing such scandals?

Father: Companies take many precautionary measures. The main cause of such leakages is the company's employees leaking the secret to other companies. To prevent this, the companies take a **'Non-Disclosure Agreement (NDA)'** from the R&D employees. This agreement imposes a heavy penalty on the defaulters. Fearing of the huge penalty the employees do not indulge in such activities.

It is advisable not to locate the R&D department near the marketing department. The employees of the marketing department will be touring always and will meet the competitor's employees during their marketing activity. Unintentionally they may reveal certain information about the new product development of his company.

It is always advisable to keep the R&D documents in a safer place and ensure out of reach of others. Some companies exhibit their innovations in exhibitions much before the product is ready for marketing. This will give time for the competitors to develop a competing model or product.

As Valluvar has said "கடைக்கொட்க" in this couplet, the innovation must be revealed only at the end i.e. when ready to go to market.

Protect the IPR - Protect the company!

6.3 Couplet: 611 / Chapter: 62
Managing Performance (ஆள் வினையுடைமை)

அருமை உடைத்தென்று அசாவாமை வேண்டும்
பெருமை முயற்சி தரும்.

Never give up a task because it is tough;
efforts bring glory.

Son: Easy to understand.

Father: Yes son. This is useful particularly for R&D. While carrying out a research project, a lot of challenges will crop up. The challenges will make the R&D man to think whether he will be able to successfully complete this project. Sometimes deciphering certain mathematical equations may pose a challenge. Sometimes certain component availability may be a challenge. The end product cost (Target Cost) fixed by the company may be a challenge to attain, particularly when the target cost is given with reference to countries like China. Pressure will mount on the R&D man. The biggest pressure will be the project completion on time. The marketing department might have fixed a launch date which has to be met. A key employee from the R&D team might have resigned creating a hurdle to the development. Getting a new hand will take a lot of time. Like this many challenges will be thrown in front of a research person. Valluvar says in such situations one should not lose heart; but must put in severe efforts. Such efforts will eventually bring success and glory.

Son: Any example of such researchers who successfully handled the challenges?

Father: I can give some examples of researchers who faced the challenges and came out successful.

- **Thomas Alwa Edison:** Edison faced over a thousand failures before successfully developing the light bulb. He famously said, "I have not failed. I've just found a thousand ways that won't work." Just imagine how much tenacity he should have got.

- **Alexander Fleming:** Fleming discovered penicillin by chance, but his subsequent efforts to purify and test it faced numerous challenges. He overcame these obstacles, revolutionizing the antibiotics.

- **J.K. Rowling:** The Harry Potter manuscript was rejected by twelve publishers. Her perseverance made the series to become a global phenomenon.

- **Wright Brothers:** They faced numerous failures and setbacks while developing the first air aircraft. Their persistence led to a successful flight in 1903.

- **Stephen Hawking:** Hawking was diagnosed with a motor neuron disease, but he continued working on black hole theory, making groundbreaking contributions despite physical limitations.

These examples demonstrate how relentless efforts can overcome challenges in innovation, leading to historic achievements and success. Valluvar was right! There were many people in history, who have faced challenges and became successful because of their untiring efforts.

Never give up - keep trying!

6.4 Couplet: 676 / Chapter: 68
Mode of execution (வினை செயல் வகை)

முடிவும் இடையூறும் முற்றியாங் கெய்தும்
படுபயனும் பார்த்துச் செயல்.

Perform by considering the target, hurdles and the benefits derived on accomplishment.

Son: Dad, Valluvar talks of performing an act. Right?

Father: Yes. But, Valluvar has told on many occasions, about the target and the final results. Here, in this couplet, he uses the word "இடையூறும்", meaning the possible failures anticipated during the process of carrying out an act, which is very important and to be noted. When he says to aim the target, he means the various targets to be adhered to while completing the job. The target may be the time limit, budget limit, compliance with technical standards etc. While trying to achieve all these targets, many obstacles may crop up. Instead of facing the obstacles when they crop up, Valluvar says, imagine and anticipate these obstacles in advance and take precautions to alleviate them. Otherwise, when the obstacles suddenly crop up, it may be too late to manage and will result in time and money loss.

In today's R&D, a terminology called **'Failure Mode Effect Analysis (FMEA)'** is used. This means anticipating the possible obstacles which may crop up to any process and taking corrective action beforehand.

There are two kinds of FMEAs.

1. Process FMEA

2. Design FMEA

Here, in this couplet we can assume that Valluvar talks of a Process FMEA because he uses the word 'செயல்' meaning process. Process FMEA is carried out in industries while deciding the production process. In businesses like Amazon, Flipkart, Swiggy etc. it is their process of offering services. In any process, FMEA can be applied. Representatives from various departments like Process, Quality, Purchase, Service etc. will be present in the FMEA meeting and everyone will deliberate the various possibilities by which the proposed process can fail. All the anticipated failure possibilities will be collectively discussed and suitable corrective actions will be decided. These corrections will be implemented in advance so that the process will not fail in the field. By using a single word 'இடையூறு' meaning 'obstacle' Valluvar emphasizes the importance of anticipating failures and taking corrective actions. This means the 'Process FMEA'. Since Valluvar has decided to use only seven words in his couplet, he can use only one appropriate word and it is up to us to elaborate and understand the correct meaning by asking questions 'what, why and how'.

He also insists that the FMEA has to be conducted focusing on achieving the 'end result' and the benefits derived thereof. The terminology 'முற்றியாங் கெய்தும் படுபயனும்' has an inner meaning that the corrective actions taken must commensurate with the eventual benefit it leads to. For example, in a production process, if the chances of failures are only meager, there is no meaning in investing huge money in preventing such rare failures.

Instead, we can live with the failure and face when it occurs. This will result in less upfront expenditure. This is a judicial decision to be taken by the management and Valluvar's thought process is the same. **Failure prevention expenses must not exceed the failure correction expenses.** But this principle may not be applicable where the failures can cause serious situations like loss of human life.

Son: Ok Dad. What are the benefits of Process FMEA?

Father: Let me list a few.

- **Improved Quality:** Identifies potential failures, reducing defects and improving overall quality.

- **Reduced Costs:** Minimizes waste, rework, and repair costs by addressing issues early.

- **Enhanced Reliability:** Increases process reliability by identifying and mitigating potential failures.

- **Increased Efficiency:** Streamlines processes, reducing downtime and increasing productivity.

By implementing Process FMEA, organisations can proactively address potential failures, improve processes, and achieve significant benefits.

Prevent obstacles by evaluating the benefits!

6.5 Couplet: 662 / Chapter: 67
Effective Performance (வினைத் திட்பம்)

ஊறொரால் உற்றபின் ஒல்காமை இவ்விரண்டின்
ஆறென்பர் ஆய்ந்தவர் கோள்.

The trait of a researcher is to take precautions against anticipated failures and not to worry if fails.

Son: Dad, the same point has already been told by Valluvar. Why again?

Father: Valluvar never repeats. The previous couplet was for a process. Here, in this couplet, he has used the word '**ஆய்ந்தவர்**' meaning a researcher. This couplet is for a research person or a designer who develops a product. Since this is addressed to a researcher, this couplet talks of **Design FMEA.**

Son: Ok Dad. How to conduct a Design FMEA?

Father: This is again carried out through a **Cross Functional Team (CFT)** meeting participated by the stakeholders like Design, Engineering, Production, Quality and Service departments. Here, the designer will present his design and all others will point out how this design can fail from each one's point of view. Such meetings will be highly sensational and will lead to arguments. The head of R&D who conducts the meeting must be a good moderator and capable of finally collecting all the valid failure possibilities to take corrective actions before finalising the design. This is important because once the design is finalised it is very difficult to modify it. If not done, a good lot of time and money may have to be spent on reworks. Many sittings of Design FMEA meetings may be necessary to eventually develop a product which will be potentially flawless.

Son: Thank you Dad for this useful explanation. I do understand how important the Design FMEA can be for a product. Can you explain to me the rest of the couplet?

Father: Valluvar is a highly practical person. He knows nothing can be 100% perfect. In spite of all precautions taken a failure may occur in the field. New product failure in the field is the worst situation that can arise for an R&D person. It will highly demotivate him. If at all, such a failure happens, Valluvar says not to worry about it, because, it had happened despite all the efforts and precautionary measures taken in advance. If a research person starts worrying about a failure, in future he cannot involve himself in any research work wholeheartedly. For this reason, Valluvar says 'not worrying after the failure (உற்றபின் ஒல்காமை) must be the trait of a research person. (ஆறென்பர் ஆய்ந்தவர் கோள்).

Normally, the initial period of product launching and shipping the products to customers is considered to be a critical period. The design department will be alert and ready to face any failure and implement any correction required in the shortest possible time. The customers should never be allowed to suffer. This is possible only when the R&D team does not get stuck with demotivation and Valluvar says to boldly face the situation.

Son: Dad, what are the advantages of Design FMEA?

Father: This has all the advantages mentioned in Process FMEA. In addition, the following benefits can be derived

- Improved Product reliability and Quality.

- Reduced Costs arising out of design changes, rework, and repairs.

- Increased Customer Satisfaction due to zero-defect products.

- Reduced Warranty Claims and savings thereof.

Envisage failures – Eliminate in advance – Ensure reliability!

Summing up the messages given above,

- Concurrent Engineering

- Process FMEA

- Design FMEA

- Intellectual Property Rights (IPR)

- Never give up R&D because it is challenging

- Never give up R&D because it has failed

Valluvar advises like a research scholar!

7

EFFECTIVE PERFORMANCE

7.0. The definition of Effective Performance

Son: Dad, it is surprising to note that a poet who lived in ancient times has written poems about 'Effective Performance'.

Father: From time immemorial, regardless of geography, an efficient performer has been successful in his life compared to a normal performer. A society, that does not have competent and skilled persons will be economically backward and suffer from poverty. Today, countries like Japan, Germany and the U.S. are considered to be highly developed because they have more percentage of skilled manpower. Beyond literacy, competency in the profession plays a major role in individual growth as well as the nation's growth. That's why Valluvar has given topmost priority to 'effective performance' in his book, Thirukkural. The names of the chapters given by him stand as proof for the kind of importance he has assigned for effective performance.

- Knowledgeable execution: (Chapter-47)
- Knowledgeable performance: (Chapter-52)
- Managing performance: (Chapter-62)
- Purity in performance: (Chapter-66)
- Effective Performance: (Chapter-67)
- Mode of execution: (Chapter-68)
- Means of making wealth: (Chapter-76)

In each chapter, he has written ten couplets and these couplets discuss the importance of effective performance and the various competencies required for an individual to be an effective performer. By writing so many couplets, Valluvar has attributed equal importance to 'effective performance' as given to 'virtuous life'.

If the performance efficiency of all the employees improves in an organisation, then, the organisation will prosper. To achieve this, the organisations today provide them with all kinds of soft skill training. These trainings focus on the elements of **"Cost, Time and Quality"**.

Now, let's explore these dimensions of effective performance as seen by Valluvar.

7.1   Couplet: 677 / Chapter: 68
Mode of execution (வினை செயல் வகை)

செய்வினை செய்வான் செயல்முறை அவ்வினை
உள்ளறிவான் உள்ளம் கொளல்.

One who wants to perform effectively learns from the one who has deep knowledge on the subject.

Son: Dad, Is it not enough if suitable training is offered to perform a job effectively?

Father: Yes. But, Valluvar says the training must be from a person who is well versed in performing the particular task. He must keep himself abreast with the latest developments in the relevant technology to teach others. If it is a project, there are experienced consulting firms who will guide in implementing the project successfully. In other words, if someone wants to accomplish any assignment or project as the case may be, he must learn it from a competent person or advisor or a consultant who is a master in the particular line. Otherwise, the chances of committing mistakes are high.

Son: Yes Dad. I understand. I will not start a job unless I am sure of doing it or till I learn it from some appropriate person. Can you give me some examples of organisations that became successful because of associating with the right consultants who were experts in the field?

Father: You know **IBM** is a big computer company. IBM hired consultants from **McKinsey** to help with their transformation in the 1990s. With McKinsey's strategies, IBM shifted its focus from hardware to services, leading to a successful turnaround. Services were not thought of as a revenue making stream earlier.

When **Jack Welch** assumed charge as the CEO of **General Electric**, the company was in bad shape. He hired consultants from **Motorola and Six Sigma** to implement the Six Sigma quality initiative. This made turn-around of the loss-making company and led to significant cost savings and efficiency improvements. This was a great turn-around story.

Apple hired consultants from **Bain & Company** to help with their 1997 restructuring. Bain's strategies helped Apple, leading to the development of many innovative products like iPod, iPhone, iPad etc.

All the above companies are already industry majors. Still, when they wanted to enter into a new domain, they took the knowledge of the experts. Valluvar's terminology 'உள்ளறிவான் உள்ளம்கொளல்' exactly means this.

Choose the experts – Use for success!

———•———

7.2   Couplet: 672 / Chapter: 68
Mode of execution (வினைசெயல்வகை)

தூங்குக தூங்கிச் செயற்பால தூங்கற்க
தூங்காது செய்யும் வினை.

**Delay the jobs which can be delayed; don't delay
the jobs which should not be delayed.**

Son: Everyone knows about this. Why a special couplet for this?

Father: It is not like that. You must see the implied meaning of this couplet. This is more for a manager rather than an executive. The word '**தூங்கி**' means delaying or postponing. In today's work environment, it is common for managers to handle multiple tasks simultaneously. During such times, instead of trying to do everything at the same time, one must prioritize the tasks and focus on completing the urgent ones first. Less urgent tasks can be delayed. This is normally known as **'Priority Assignment'**

I've seen employees who fail to understand this concept and waste time on non-essential tasks, only to work until midnight to complete critical tasks. When multiple tasks pile up, they decide based on a **'first cum first served'** basis and carry out the task which arrived first rather than prioritizing based on the importance of the task. This is where the problem starts.

For instance, a manager may assign an employee to complete a particular job at the closing hours of the office, just before the executive is ready to leave for the day. Now, the executive has to work late hours to complete it. Had the priority been told, the employee might have completed the priority job on time before the closing hours. Here **'priority assignment'** is important. This is the implied meaning of this couplet. To avoid this, many supervisors label the tasks as 'urgent' or 'priority' when assigning the work to subordinates. Some organisations use colour coding, such as red, to indicate high-priority tasks.

Valluvar's couplet emphasizes the importance of prioritizing tasks to avoid delays and ensure efficient management.

Prioritize and be on time!

7.3 Couplet: 668 / Chapter: 67
Effective Performance (வினைத் திட்பம்)

கலங்காது கண்ட வினைக்கண் துளங்காது
தூக்கம் கடிந்து செயல்.

Once decided without ambiguity, complete the job without further delay"

Son: Deciding a job without ambiguity is ok. Why it must be implemented immediately? If implemented after some time what happens?

Father: In today's management, taking clear business decisions without ambiguity is crucial for any business. Taking such decisions can be challenging, especially when multiple factors which are beyond the control of the decision-taking authority need to be considered. This requires smart data analysis with protracted results. Normally a team will work on this. That's why collective decisions made in meetings are often more effective than individual decisions. Valluvar insists that the decisions taken must be clear and without any ambiguity.

Many times calculations are made considering the present situations like exchange rates, steel prices etc. When such assumptions are made based on certain variables, delaying the implementation can give an opportunity for the assumptions to go wrong. It will hinder the success of the project. Therefore, once the project is decided it is better to implement it at the earliest without giving a chance for the variables to vary and affect the calculations made. In addition, this is more relevant in today's competitive business world, where circumstances can change rapidly. Any delay may allow the competition to enter causing a threat. Every minute is important in business and delaying can affect the business.

Son: Dad, Can you explain some situations where delayed decisions lead to failures?

Father: I can give you so many practical examples

Once, a company decided to recruit a competent head for its R&D department. Getting such a rare candidate is difficult. The HR department took a lot of efforts and shortlisted a few candidates and finally, the management team selected one good candidate. However, there was a delay in preparing the offer, routing it through proper channels and getting the signature of the CEO. This took two weeks of time. By this time the candidate got another job and joined another company. This was a big setback for the company which had a lot of R&D development plans.

In another case, the company wanted to exhibit its products in an international exhibition and made extensive preparations. The organisers of the exhibition have prescribed certain formalities and a time frame for enrolling to the exhibition. However, the administration department of the company delayed by following certain internal approval formalities and by that time all the stalls in the exhibition had sold out. The company could not exhibit its products in the exhibition and faced severe business loss.

Here is another example which happens in most of the industries. A company delayed addressing an employee's genuine concerns. The employee wanted to quit but was willing to continue if his concerns were addressed. The management also has decided to consider his grievances favorably. But, an abnormal delay in implementing it created doubt in the mind of the employee and he joined the competitor, creating a big setback for the organisation.

Like this many examples can be given. Any couplet of Valluvar will carry a meaning which is deep in nature and can be understood only when probed. Advice by a poet who lived two thousand years ago to 'not to delay' and 'to act swiftly' after making a decision showcases his visionary thinking.

Delayed implementation gives room for changes!

———•—

7.4 Couplet: 670 / Chapter: 67
Effective Performance (வினைத் திட்பம்)

எனைத்திட்பம் எய்தியக் கண்ணும் வினைத்திட்பம்
வேண்டாரை வேண்டாது உலகு.

Despite having all competencies, if unable to complete a job effectively, he gets rejected.

Son: Dad, Can you explain this couplet to me?

Father: Yes son. Any amount of knowledge, intelligence or hard work one possesses will be a waste unless these characters enable him to complete a task successfully without any flaw.

I can give you an example. There is a football player in the forward position. He handles the ball very well. He can dribble, manipulate and manage the ball very efficiently, mesmerising the audience. Valluvar says unless he is able to shoot a goal he will not find a place in the team next time.

Another example: An employee is punctual, regular to work, never takes a day off without a reason, and also well disciplined. But, when assigned a task, he is lazy and slow and requires guidance every time. The company does not want such persons.

Similarly, you will find a lot of people in the society having good qualifications but are unable to complete their jobs effectively.

Son: Ok Dad. Let it be. Then what is the solution? Can we terminate them from employment?

Father: No. Definitely not. The individual must be made to understand his shortcomings and must be enabled to learn the skills required for effective performance. Or, the organisation must identify such employees' shortcomings (**Gap Analysis**) and provide the necessary training to improve. This will include soft skill training to enhance their performance. It's easier to 'upskill' an existing employee than to hire and train a new one. There are many organisations which exclusively offer such training services. Utilizing these services will be highly beneficial.

In this couplet, Valluvar categorically says that a poor performer becomes unwanted, even if he possesses many other good qualities. True. An organisation cannot carry empty wagons.

Effective Performance excels other qualities!

7.5 Couplet: 640 / Chapter: 64
Ministry (அமைச்சு)

முறைப்படச் சூழ்ந்தும் முடிவிலவே செய்வர்
திறப்பாடு இலாஅ தவர்.

Incompetency leads to incomplete jobs despite adhering to all procedures.

Son: Here also Valluvar talks of competency in the job.

Father: Yes son. In the previous couplet he explained that despite having many good qualifications if one cannot effectively complete a job then he is not required in the organization. In this couplet he says even if a person follows all the systems and procedures very well unless he is competent to complete the job, then he will fail.

A typical example would be a doctor in operation theatre. He would have followed all the pre-requirements and procedures required like hand hygiene, wearing sterile gloves, personal protective equipment (PPE), wearing masks, caps, gowns, eye protection, patient identification procedures, anesthesia preparation, ESU safety etc. But, unless he knows thoroughly the step-by-step procedure of carrying out the operation, he will fail. All the preparations he made will not help.

It is applicable to other tasks also. Valluvar once again indirectly insists on giving thorough 'on the job training'. Many companies have a 'full pledged' training centre where all necessary infrastructure has been established to train the employees and prepare them for successfully carrying out the job proposed for them.

Son: Is it not followed in all industries?

Father: Most of the organisations induct a new employee into the job by attaching him to a senior employee and expect the senior employee to teach the job. In such cases normally the expected training will not happen. If at all it happens, it does not happen effectively. Exclusive training in carrying out a job is the inner meaning of this couplet.

Training first and Job next!

7.6   Couplet: 483 / Chapter: 49
Right Timing (காலமறிதல்)

அருவினை என்ப உளவோ கருவியான்
காலம் அறிந்து செயின்?

***Is there any impossible task, if the right tool is deployed
at the right time?***

Son: Dad, This couplet is very simple.

Father: Yes. Apparently, the couplet tells a simple point. But, in reality, there is a great meaning in it. There are many companies which became successful only because they used the right tool at the right time.

Google Pay (G Pay) in India is indeed a remarkable success story to demonstrate this couplet. The success can be attributed to:

The Right Time: Google Pay was launched in India in 2017, coinciding with the country's push towards digital payments after the implementation of demonetization, when everyone wanted to reduce physical cash transactions. This was the 'right time' for G Pay to launch its operation in India.

The right tool (கருவி): Google Pay which developed the best user friendly software tied up with most of the banks in India and with appropriate payment processors like NPCI. This enabled seamless cash transfers. More than everything the software was so user friendly that even less educated masses could easily use this app. Besides, this app supported many forms of payments like UPI, credit/debit cards, and net banking. In addition G Pay was continuously innovating new ideas based on customer feedback.

JIO: The timing of the JIO launch was perfect when the Indian population was looking for 4G services in 2016. The right technology from global tech leaders Samsung and Ericsson for infrastructure development was tied up.

UBER: Uber's success could be another example of Valluvar's couplet for its timely expansion in the Indian market in 2013 with the best possible software tool which made everyone's commuting experience an easy one.

Like this, so many examples can be given.

Son: Dad, I am thrilled by your examples. Valluvar uses a word 'அருவினை' in this couplet. Can you explain the relevance here?

Father: 'அருவினை' means rare accomplishments. Valluvar says if these two factors i-e the right tool and tight timing are combined one can accomplish rare jobs. No one can deny that **G Pay, Jio and Uber** are rarest of the rare accomplishments and were possible only because of the usage of the right tools (software) at the right time.

Using the right tool at the right time can create history!

7.7   Couplet: 490 / Chapter: 49
Right Timing (காலமறிதல்)

கொக்கொக்க கூம்பும் பருவத்து மற்றதன்
குத்தொக்க சீர்த்த விடத்து.

***Like a crane awaiting the right prey, one must
await the ripe juncture to act.***

Son: Dad, Valluvar always gives apt examples.

Father: Yes. Normally the crane will await its prey without even a small jiggle on the brink of a stream till it spots the right fish to catch. In this couplet, Valluvar emphasizes two points. One point is that whenever someone is waiting for the right time to execute a job, he must maintain the **utmost calmness and secrecy**. No noise must be made. No information must leak. This is applicable to critical operations like capturing enemies, terrorists, culprits etc. This is also applicable to clinch a business deal without exposing it to competitors. Another fitting example will be while launching a new product in the market. Absolute secrecy takes the competitor by surprise. By citing the example of a 'crane' Valluvar insists on secrecy and confidentiality to be maintained before encashing an opportunity.

The second point he makes is that a time that **yields the best results** must be chosen. Again the crane example reveals a point. The crane will allow all the small fishes to pass by. The moment a big fish is spotted, immediately it swings into action and picks it up. Therefore, the right timing is the time that gives the best score in business. Many examples can be given for this statement.

- **Steve Jobs** saw great potential for personal computers, grabbed the opportunity and created a history in the computing field.

- **Jeff Bezos** saw an opportunity in e-commerce and used it through Amazon for online shopping.

- **Mammen Mappillai** saw great potential for tyres in the Indian market and became a pioneer in Tyre making in India.

- **DhirubaiAmbani** saw a great future for Textiles in India and rightly grabbed at the right moment.

Festive seasons like Christmas in Europe, Diwali in India, and Pongal in Tamil Nadu are seasonal market timings, which, every business person avails to maximize his sales. Selling textbooks during school opening times can be another example.

Son: Can you give me some examples of who started at the wrong time and failed?

Normally I do not want to give failure examples for aspiring entrepreneurs like you. Still, I can give an example. A typical example is 'Hitler' who started his war against Russia called **'Operation Barbarossa'** in a severe winter (-20 to -30 degrees celsius) which his soldiers could not tolerate. They starved for want of food which could not be moved to them due to bad weather conditions. This timing of initiating a war against Russia was bad and was one of the major reasons for his defeat.

The right time for the right action matters!

7.8   Couplet: 673 / Chapter: 68
Mode of execution (வினை செயல் வகை)

ஒல்லும்வாய் எல்லாம் வினை நன்றே ஒல்லாக்கால்
செல்லும்வாய் நோக்கிச் செயல்.

Whenever possible carry on the job; If not, at least make progress towards the goal.

Son: Dad, this is a common piece of advice to move ahead if stuck for some reason. In industry parlance can you explain me?

Father: This applies to big projects. Whenever some big projects are undertaken, it involves many activities like Material Planning, Procurement, Logistics, Installation, Testing, Trial Run etc. All these activities must be coordinated well for successfully completing the project. Since the project contains many activities, the possibilities of delays from the suppliers, delays from the government for various approvals, and delays due to various other factors may affect the project. I have seen many projects getting stopped in between and lying idle for years due to some reasons.

Valluvar says under such circumstances it is better to carry on at least some possible activities towards the goal instead of keeping the project totally shut. Thus, the project will be kept alive so that it is easy to restart once the obstacle gets cleared.

Keep going even during hurdles!

7.9   Couplet: 489 / Chapter: 49
Right Timing (காலமறிதல்)

எய்தற்கு அரியது இயைந்தக்கால் அந்நிலையே
செய்தற்கு அரிய செயல்.

If the right opportunity comes up that is the right time to complete even a rare job.

Son: How to decide which is the right time to carry out a job?

Father: The right time to complete a task is the moment when all necessary resources, tools, environment etc. fall in place in favour of completing a task. When such an opportunity arises, Valluvar says, one should not postpone the task for other reasons. This holds good for business also, particularly for acquisitions and mergers.

Son: Can you give me some examples of missed opportunities in business?

Father: Yes son. I can give you many examples.

- **Blockbuster** declined Netflix's acquisition offer of 50 million$ in the year 2000. Netflix's market value rose to 250 billion$ in 2022. Blockbuster missed the great opportunity and became bankrupt in 2010.

- **Google** turned down Instagram's acquisition offer for 100 million$ in the year 2011. But, Facebook acquired Instagram for 1.0 billion$ in 2012. Instagram's value exceeded 150 billion$ in 2022. Google missed the opportunity.

- **Nokia** rejected the Android partnership in 2005. Nokia's market share went down from 40% to 3% by 2013. But Android dominated the global smartphone market with more than 70% market share.

Similarly, there are many instances that can be cited for missing opportunities.

Besides big business events I can also give you some examples from day-to-day happenings to demonstrate this point.

Let us assume a child requires an eye surgery. An eye specialist visits the town where the child resides. This is an opportunity to get the child treated. The opportunity should not be missed at any cost. But I have seen people missing such an opportunity due to other commitments like weddings, examinations etc.

Another example that I have personally witnessed. A candidate from India received a scholarship to study abroad at a good university, which covers all the expenses required for the study. But this candidate consulted an astrologer (In India this system of referring to an astrologer before taking a crucial decision still prevails), who advised him against traveling overseas due to unfavorable star positions. The candidate developed fear and declined the offer.

In contrast, his friend, undeterred by similar concerns grabbed the opportunity and even skipped his own sister's wedding and decided to pursue the scholarship. Years later, he achieved great success and prosperity in life and could buy a new house for his sister, while the other person remained ordinary, regretting his decision.

This story reconfirms Valluvar's teaching that the right opportunity should never be missed.

Missed opportunity may not return!

Summing up the messages given above,

- Learn from the experienced.

- Prioritize jobs.

- Definition of perfect execution of a task.

- Importance of competency in the job.

- Incompetency leads to incomplete jobs.

- The right tool at the right time leads to rare accomplishments.

- Keep calm till the right opportunity comes.

- The right opportunity is the one which gives the best results.

- Do not totally stop for temporary hurdles.

- Never miss a ripe opportunity.

Effective performance is the essence of success!

MOTIVATION

8. Motivation redefined

Son: Many leading motivational speakers have spoken about motivation. Is there anything special in Thirukkural?

Father: The human mind is an incredibly powerful one. If anyone is determined to carry out a task, he can achieve it irrespective of the toughness or complexity of the job. Many examples can be given to prove this. In today's competitive business world, only those with mental courage can achieve success. Not only the heads of organisations but also all employees must have the same winning 'mindset' for the organisation to succeed.

Famous motivational authors like Kopmeyer and Dale Carnegie have written many books about the power of the mind and how to use it to achieve great success in life. However, the great Valluvar has explained the power of the mind in a different way in many of his couplets. He emphasizes that a powerful mind is an essential character for any individual to become successful in life. He also draws a line between other competencies and a powerful mind to achieve great heights in life. Let's look at a few of these couplets.

—·•·—

8.1 Couplet: 619 / Chapter: 62
Managing Performance (ஆள் வினையுடைமை)

தெய்வத்தான் ஆகாது எனினும் முயற்சிதன்
மெய்வருத்தக் கூலி தரும்.

Even if God declines, one's efforts with hard work will yield results.

Son: How come, dad, when God declines one can be successful?

Father: This is only to motivate people that anyone can accomplish even impossible tasks with hard work and relentless efforts. Valluvar wants to emphasize the magnitude of the 'mental power' of human beings by using this unique terminology.

Son: For motivating people this may be taken as advice. Do you think this will really work?

Father: Yes son. Valluvar never tells anything that is impossible. See the following examples for yourself and decide.

Nick Vujicic, an Australian, was born without both the hands and legs. He was a bundle of flesh having all other organs intact. In fact, he was abandoned by God. His mother thought of doing away with him foreseeing the hardships he will face in his life. But the story was different. As he grew he could develop a strong mind and he decided to face the world. He never allowed his handicap to demotivate him. In reality, he challenged the creator. He developed such a powerful mind and grew in his career and started advocating the same powerful mind to everyone. He became a renowned motivational speaker, travelling to more than 160 countries. He got married and has four children. In his case, it is proved that "Even if God declines, one's efforts with hard work will yield results"

Similarly, **Lizzie Velasquez**, an American lady, had a rare congenital condition that affected her physical appearance. She was considered to be one of the ugliest women in the world. She spent many days in isolation crying about her condition. God has abandoned her in the society. Despite being ridiculed and bullied, she became world-famous through her book 'Lizzie Beautiful'. Not only that she became famous through her book, but she also became a successful motivational speaker. When she speaks on the stage, the audiences are carried away by her powerful speech and ignore her face. Here too Valluvar's words are proved.

Helen Keller born in 1880 became blind and deaf at young age itself due to severe illness. Despite this challenge, with the help of her teacher Anne Sullivan she learned to communicate through touch and was able to write also. She graduated at the age of twenty four and became an advocate for the handicapped, became a lecturer, and also a political activist. Above all, she has written twelve books and created a history.

There are many more examples of such successes. Son, you must understand that if a person decides to achieve, he can achieve anything through his determination and hard work. Let mankind develop such courage to accomplish things for the betterment of society.

Son: Sorry Dad. I doubted Valluvar's words. I could understand that he has written this couplet only to motivate people and make them achievers.

God proposes – Man disposes!

———•———

8.2 Couplet: 772 / Chapter: 78
Glory of Army (படைச் செருக்கு)

கான முயலெய்த அம்பினில் யானை
பிழைத்த வேல் ஏந்தல் இனிது.

***Better to carry a spear which misses an elephant
rather than an arrow which kills a rabbit.***

Son: Dad, this couplet is interesting. Valluvar talks about hunting in a forest.

Father: Yes. He talks about goal setting in life. In India, I have seen the elders advising youngsters to start any venture in a small way and grow bigger as time passes. But, Valluvar says to aim high even if you fail. Instead of accurately aiming a rabbit in a forest he says aim an elephant even if you miss it. He talks of courage here and we can take his advice here as a matter of 'business courage'.

Son: Is it not risky to start a big business to start with?

Father: No. Here you have to take the example of Chinese. They plan any business in a big way keeping the global market in mind. Because of this, their overheads are getting shared over huge volumes and the selling price becomes extremely competitive. Naturally, they have become successful globally. Such high-aiming people even if they face certain setbacks or failures initially, they will win eventually. This has been proved today in the 21st century. This requires business courage to venture. One must take calculated risks in business.

If a student aims to get 100% in his examinations he may get 90% or 80%. On the other hand, if a student's aim itself is 40% just to get a pass, he will get less than 40% and eventually fail in his examinations. Aiming high is always better.

In business also we always keep the Annual Targets at least at 20% more than the normal calculated target. Then only, we can expect to finish at 100%.

Son: Can you give me some examples of companies who have set high targets and became successful?

Father: Toyota is one good example for setting very high quality and productivity norms and achieving it. In this process, they have developed many quality systems like TPM, Six Sigma, JIT, Kaizen, Poke Yoke etc. which are being used by many industries globally to improve their quality and productivity.

Another example is **Tesla's** target of 500,000 electric vehicles per year. This was a huge figure and Tesla could achieve it.

Like this, **Pfizer** set a rapid development goal for the COVID-19 vaccine and it did achieve the same.

All these examples demonstrate aiming high is always better and Valluvar advocates this principle for all of us for any activity.

Aim high - achieve high!

8.3   Couplet: 612 / Chapter: 63
Managing Performance (ஆள்வினை யுடைமை)

வினைக்கண் வினைகெடல் ஓம்பல் வினைக்குறை
தீர்ந்தாரின் தீர்ந்தன்று உலகு.

***After eying a job to be tough, anyone quitting
will be discarded by the society.***

Son: When a job is very tough to finish why one should not decide to leave the job?

Father: Here, Valluvar does not want anyone to stop the job halfway. Had he applied his mind before starting the job and sensed the toughness he should have not started it. That is why in the earlier couplets, Valluvar has insisted on thinking well before starting an act and evaluating own strength before embarking on a project. If all his advices were taken care of and in spite of that, if any hurdle comes on the way, Valluvar says emphatically not to quit the task in between. One reason for this statement is to motivate him to complete the job at any cost.

The other reason is the society. Shelving a project in between will spread a negative image all around. The financiers will hesitate to finance him. The employees may feel demotivated and in some companies, the employees even leave the organisation because they start feeling unsecured. The material suppliers may hesitate to supply materials on credit. All these situations will arise due to the fact that the project was terminated in between.

This kind of losing faith is like an infectious disease and spreads around easily. Having understood this aspect Valluvar says once you start a job, never quit in between because it causes invisible damage to one's reputation.

Think well before starting and be firm in not quitting!

8.4 Kutal: 666 / Chapter: 67
Effective Performance (விளைத் திட்பம்)

எண்ணிய எண்ணியாங்கு எய்துப எண்ணியார்
திண்ணியர் ஆகப் பெறின்.

***The one with mental determination performs
exactly as planned.***

Son: Dad, Here Valluvar talks of having a powerful mind. Is it not?

Father: Yes. But his focus is on completing a job exactly as planned 'எண்ணியாங்கு'. Making a movie will be an apt example for this couplet. The director must finish the movie in the same way it was imagined by him. Then only it can be called successful.

Since we discuss an industrial subject, let us take an industrial project for example. This project may have many parameters to be complied with, for its successful completion as given below.

- Meeting the Functional requirements

- Meeting the technical specifications

- Delivering the quality specified

- Completing within the estimated Project cost

- Completing within the Project Scheduled timing

- etc.

Normally all the above parameters will be discussed in advance in various meetings for successfully achieving all these parameters. Detailed planning (எண்ணிய) will be done by the execution team.

On completion of the project, all the above parameters must have been achieved without any deviation from the planning.

If the project has to be completed as planned without any deviation it requires a tremendous amount of professional willpower to integrate the various aspects of the project, like materials, manpower, machinery, hardware, software etc.

Valluvar says only a person having such willpower can complete the job as meticulously as planned. This may be an industrial project, making a cinema or writing a book. Everything requires planning and execution and above all the willpower to achieve it.

Determination is the key to achieve exact performance!

8.5 Couplet: 593 / Chapter: 60
Motivation (ஊக்கமுடைமை)

ஆக்கம் இழந்தேமென்று அல்லாவார் ஊக்கம்
ஒருவந்தம் கைத்துடை யார்.

***The one who has motivation built within him will not
get dejected even when facing failures.***

Son: Once again Valluvar is motivating us.

Father: Yes son. Most of the time, when one faces failures he gets demotivated and goes into failure mode. This must never be allowed. Valuvar says the one who has motivation built with in him will not worry about failures. He will bounce back and win.

I can give you some examples of companies that bounced back after terrible failures.

Apple went to nearly a bankrupt state in 1997. It was the perseverance of Steve Jobs who revitalized the company and made it a great success.

In the year 2009, **General Motors** went to bankruptcy. It was the sole effort of Jack Welch who completely revamped the entire operations and brought it back to success.

In the year 2006, **Ford Motors** was at a $12.7 billion loss. Ford also bounced back with new models and cost-cutting measures.

In India, **Royal Enfield** the two-wheeler division of Eicher Motors, faced severe loss and the father Mr.VikramLal wanted to close down the division. But his son SiddarthaLal, who then returned from London after finishing his degree in automotive technology sought two years of time from his father to correct the situation. Father agreed. During this period SiddharthaLal made tremendous efforts in re-designing the two-wheeler motorcycle and he launched a new model in the name and style of 'Thunder Bird' which became a great success. Afterwards, many innovative models were launched by him and the company created history in the two-wheeler segment by transforming the share value of the company from Indian Rs.22/- to Rs.19000/-.

There are many examples of Valluvar's claim that the one who has the determination will not bother about failures and at the same time fight back to achieve success.

'Self-motivated' seldom fails!

8.6 Couplet: 661 / Chapter: 67
Effective Performance (விளைத் திட்பம்)

வினைத்திட்பம் என்ப தொருவன் மனத்திட்பம்
மற்றைய எல்லாம் பிற.

**Effective performance is a mental factor
others no matter.**

Son: This couplet is like the saying 'if there is a will there is a way'. Am I right Dad?

Father: Yes. More or less you are right. Performing a job effectively requires mental courage. Such courage gives the necessary willpower for planning, timely execution and facing challenges if any.

A company may have all the necessary infrastructure for accomplishing a project. But, unless the company has the right manpower, who are willing to tackle any problem and face hardships, the project cannot be completed successfully. There is a saying that 'man makes the difference'. Particularly the top man must have the right attitude or willpower.

Son: How do you define the willpower?

Father: All human beings are not the same while accomplishing a task. There are people, who understand the job thoroughly before starting, plan the job meticulously, plan the material required, plan the correct manpower required, plan the correct tool to be used, decide the method of execution and perfectly coordinate all these activities to complete a job on time and exactly as planned. Above all, these kinds of persons will be ready to face any challenge which arises during the course of implementation and will become successful. They will never leave any job unfinished at any point of time. All these qualities represent the 'willpower' of an individual. Even an average intelligent person can succeed if he has willpower. Even a less qualified person can win if he has mental willpower. Even a handicapped person can win if he has willpower. This is what Valluvar means by the terminology 'மற்றைய எல்லாம் பிற' in Tamil.

Today, I see in India, the parents give top priority for the marks or the grades the children will get in the school instead of enhancing their willpower by training them on perseverance, motivation, effort, timing, perfection, quality etc. (மனத்திட்பம்). These parents force their children in academic marks and most of the children memorize the subject to get high marks. This is the reason why the most successful people are not from the top rankers. Only the mid-ranking students that too who study through their mother tongue excel in life.

Therefore, one should strive hard from his young age to develop the mental willpower to achieve greater heights in life. According to me getting an education in one's mother tongue enhances the understanding of the subjects well and this understanding increases the competency of the students.

Son: Dad, any example of such successful people?

Father: Yes. Many examples can be given. I am giving a few here

Mahatma Gandhi: He is an example of great 'willpower'. He had to face the powerful British Empire which was ruling the world in the 1930s. Mahatma Gandhi dared to oppose them and faced many challenges and threats. He did not budge and finally achieved freedom for India.

Like this, there are many more names like Albert Einstein, Walt Disney, and Nelson Mandela who won because of their 'willpower'.

'Will-Power' wins always!

8.7 Couplet: 620 / Chapter: 62
Managing Performance (ஆள் வினை யுடைமை)

ஊழையும் உப்பக்கம் காண்பர் உலைவின்றித்
தாழாது உருற்று பவர்.

He who puts his efforts relentlessly without fear will chase and see off the destiny.

Son: Great dad! Highly encouraging words.

Father: Yes son. Valluvar attaches a lot of importance to fearlessness and untiring efforts.

Son: How can a person change the destiny, Dad?

Father: To be frank with you, no one really knows what destiny is before something happens. If destiny is known beforehand no one will try anything and the whole world will come to a standstill. The word destiny is used after something happens. Whenever there is a failure even after sincere efforts by someone, the elderly people around him use the word 'destiny' to pacify him. Otherwise, he will blame himself for the failure and go into demotivation. He will be repenting lifelong. This is not good for an individual. This is more intense if the failure is a major one. Therefore the word destiny is used to pacify failures happening due to unknown reasons or despite best efforts.

But, shockingly, people have started attributing destiny even to very small failures. This has become a convenient escape route for those who are not willing to put in effort. This has started hampering the personal growth of the individual and also the society's growth. Valluvar steps in here and tells everyone, that, they can win over destiny if they put in fearless and relentless efforts. Here, he means the fear of destiny. Destiny, the invisible subject, if allowed to enter into one's mind, can create fear, even if he is a strong-willed person.

But society in general has accepted the existence of destiny and many people strongly believe that everything happens as per destiny. Even if a person has succeeded due to his hard work, the people attribute his hard work itself was because of destiny. Instead of arguing, Valluvar has given a solution. He says relentless efforts will see off destiny and let us accept and put in efforts to succeed.

Forget destiny and rely on your efforts!

— • ● • —

Summing up the messages given above,

In one couplet Valluvar says that **'relentless efforts'** will lead to success. In another couplet Valluvar says **'mental determination'** will lead to success. Yet in another couplet he says **'hard work'** will lead to success. If a person follows relentless work automatically he will get determination and hard work. Similarly, if a person works hard he will automatically get determination and effort.

Or, if any one of the above criteria is followed the other two will automatically follow. Let us at least follow one of the three characters to be successful in life! Valluvar also says in addition to having such characters, one must always set a high goal for himself, and he should never leave a job unfinished at any cost. Valluvar wants everyone to be nothing short of a great performer.

Valluvar the best motivator!

9

EFFECTIVE COMMUNICATION

9.0. The importance of 'communication' in business

Son: Dad, I am eager to know what Valluvar has told on 'effective communication'.

Father: Though Valluvar has written a separate chapter for effective communication, he has talked about communication in other chapters also. Why Valluvar has given so much importance to 'communication'? Many people in the history have changed the society through their speeches. Some personalities have changed the kingdoms and rulers using their oratory skills. A typical example will be Hitler. He could speak in such a way as to touch the emotions of the audience and attract them to join his movement even though his party's ideology was not an admirable one. Abraham Lincoln, Winston Churchill and Martin Luther King were also great orators in those days and conquered the minds of people. In India, C.N.Annadurai, shortly called 'Anna' was a spellbound orator both in English and Tamil who changed the Congress-led government using his mesmerising oratory skills. He attracted millions of youngsters through his speech.

Valluvar, in one of his couplets defines how an oratory speech must be.

கேட்டார் பிணிக்கும் தகைவாய்க் கேளாரும்
வேட்ப மொழிவதாம் சொல். (குறள் - 643)

An oration must bind the audience to the speaker and make those who missed it long for hearing it. (couplet - 643)

We cannot assume that all the couplets of Valluvar on "effective communication' teaches only public oration. More than public speaking, Valluvar focuses on official communications. In today's business world, effective communication has fetched millions worth of business. Only for this reason, many organisations depute the right communicator to attend a particular business deal that faces severe competition.

Not only in 'one-to-one' meetings but also in business meetings, though the subject knowledge is important, presenting the knowledge with supporting data and statistics makes a difference. The body language, the selection of words, and the tone used to communicate must be so attractive that the participants in the meeting start admiring the speech and heed to the points made.

In a nutshell, Valluvar says that effective communication is very important for one's success whether in politics or business. Now, let us see some of his kurls on Effective Communication.

9.1   Couplet: 722 / Chapter: 73
Courage in forums (அவையஞ்சாமை)

கற்றாருள் கற்றார் எனப்படுவர் கற்றார்முன்
கற்ற செலச் சொல்லு வார்.

***Those who could drive home a point to a learned
gathering will be termed as learned among the learned.***

Son: Dad, This couplet defines the glory of a good communicator.

Father: Yes. Effective communication is the backbone of any successful business. Every transaction in the business takes place through communication either verbal or written. It enables organisations to convey their vision, build strong relationships, and achieve results. Clear and concise communication builds collaboration, avoids conflicts, and ensures frictionless execution. Because of this unwanted debates are eliminated and productive time increases. It boosts productivity and efficiency, enhances employee engagement and develops customer satisfaction.

Today, numerous meetings, technology-specific seminars and discussion groups take place globally. Top experts from around the world participate in these intellectual gatherings. To attend such knowledge-sharing events, organisations pertaining to industries, businesses, hospitals, universities etc. select and sponsor eligible employees. Anyone representing his organisation must effectively present his ideas and drive home the point he wants to make, to the learned gathering. Such successful participation not only earns him recognition as 'learned among the learned' but also enhances the reputation of the organisation which he represents. However, if a highly knowledgeable and skilled individual in an organisation lacks effective communication skills to present his expertise in a gathering of scholars, then his capabilities become handicapped. Thus, in this couplet, Valluvar emphasizes the importance of effective communication to an intellectual gathering.

Son: Thank you for your clarifications, Dad! Why such an important subject is not found in today's school syllabus?

Father: Yes. In many schools, it is not taught. Particularly in India, the parents want their children to get high marks in the subjects. They do not give priority to sports, extracurricular activities, public speaking etc. I will say mostly no parent thinks about the communication capabilities of their children.

But, after reading this couplet, I realize that, for children to succeed in a competitive world, their communication capability must be developed at their young age itself. Not only the capability of addressing a gathering but also the capability of day-to-day transactions in the schools has to improve.

Parents to watch!

---•---

9.2   Couplet: 647 / Chapter: 65
Effective Communication (சொல் வன்மை)

சொலல் வல்லன் சோர்விலன் அஞ்சானவனை
இகல்வெல்லல் யார்க்கும் அரிது.

It is impossible to win the one who is a good communicator, not lazy and fearless.

Son: Here Valluvar gives three important qualities of a winning personality. Am I right dad? Can you explain what exactly a 'good communicator' means in business?

Father: It refers to a communicator who effectively conveys his ideas and thoughts to others, ensuring they are correctly understood. Effective communication is crucial in today's business, whether written or verbal and applies to interactions with everyone connected with a business like superiors, subordinates, suppliers, customers etc.

This means one must clearly express his intended message, avoiding ambiguity. The words used should not lead to dual meanings. On many occasions, I have seen arguments arising out of 'misunderstood conversations'. In the business world, particularly when making agreements between two parties which may be related to purchases, sales, marketing, exports, projects etc. precise and unambiguous language is essential to avoid misinterpretation. I have seen a lot of litigations in the courts purely because of ambiguous agreements. Therefore, the meaning of the terminology 'good communicator' in this couplet must be taken as an individual who can effectively communicate without ambiguity at any point of time.

Son: Dad, what is the meaning of "சோர்விலன்" in this couplet?

Father: This terminology means "without laziness". Lazy people can never be winners. Even if he is an intelligent and well-qualified person, if he is lazy, he can never be a winner. I understand that reacting fast to any situation is an indication of not being lazy. Not being lazy is reflected in actions like immediate response, quick decisions and speedy completion of jobs. Laziness often leads to poor quality and delayed delivery.

Son: Valluvar talks of fearlessness as a character. For success why this character is required? Communication and 'not being lazy' is ok. Why fearlessness?

Father: Here, fear does not mean fearing about someone. It is the quality of taking risks. Many people will fear to take risks. In business, one must take calculated risks. I have seen many people losing business opportunities simply because of fear of failure. If one applies his mind with proper data analysis, he can take well calculated risks without any fear of losing.

Also one should not fear competition. In any business every player whether big or small will have his own market share. Benz car has its market share while Maruti car also sells substantially. Business courage will make even small players to encroach into big player's domain. Valluvar says 'business courage' will lead to success.

Son: Ok Dad. I will follow Valluvar's advice and try to develop my communication skills, try to be alert without giving room for laziness and also I will develop my business courage.

Be smart and be a winner!

9.3   Couplet: 648 / Chapter: 65
Effective Communication (சொல் வன்மை)

விரைந்து தொழில்கேட்கும் ஞாலம் நிரந்தினிது
சொல்லுதல் வல்லார்ப் பெறின்.

Everyone will be eager to receive a task from the one who explains well with a smiling face.

Son: Dad, Valluvar uses the word 'ஞாலம்' here. The meaning of this word is **'world'** isn't it?

Father: In many of his couplets, Valluvar has used a word equivalent to 'world'. But, in most of the cases, the word does not mean the world; it denotes the society or the people living in that locality. Here, in this couplet, it means the employees working in that workplace. This couplet is mainly written for the people who are in a position to assign jobs (supervisors) to their subordinates. Valluvar says while assigning a job to the subordinates the supervisor must explain the method of executing the job preferably sequentially. Also, Valluvar adds that the job should not be assigned in a commanding tone; instead, it must be communicated with a smiling face. If this is followed by a supervisor all the employees will show eagerness to receive an assignment from him.

There is a saying. **'A job well defined is half done'**. The word 'நிரந்து ' used in this couplet exactly means a 'well defined' job.

Son: Dad, How to define a job correctly?

Father: It depends on the nature of the job. Still, I can give certain points which are generally important to define a job.

- Job specifications.

- Quality requirements.

- Standards to be complied.

- Procedure to be followed.

- Special tools to be used.

- Time to complete etc.

Besides these points, if the supervisor can indicate the possible challenges one may face in accomplishing the job it helps the subordinate to prepare himself fully for the job. Above all, if all these details are given with a smiling face (நிரந்தினிது), it makes a lot of difference and will motivate the subordinate towards timely completion with good quality.

Any shortage of information on the above will result in a rework. Rework is time-consuming and expensive. It spoils the morale of an organisation.

Sub-delegate with smiles – make everyone to perform!

9.4   Couplet: 725 / Chapter: 73
Courage in a forum (அவையஞ்சாமை)

ஆற்றின் அளவறிந்து கற்க அவையஞ்சா
மாற்றம் கொடுத்தற் பொருட்டு.

Prepare for a meeting understanding depth of the subject, convey courageously, in such a way to bring in a change.

Son: Great Dad. Valluvar advises on facing a meeting where learned people are assembled. Right? Can you tell me how to prepare for such an important meeting?

Father: Valluvar says that one has to fully understand the subject of the proposed meeting and prepare well to attend the meeting. Valluvar also says that he must convey the prepared subject without any fear in such a way to make an impact that brings in a change in the minds of the participants. What an excellent advice to follow! This means the preparation must be thorough.

Son: Dad, can you tell me how to prepare my speech for a meeting?

Father:I will suggest the following points to effectively prepare for a meeting.

- Understand the subject thoroughly. This requires an in-depth reading or research. Lots of data may have to be collected, analyzed, and interpreted and certain impressive decisions should be arrived at for demonstrating in the meeting. The decisions arrived at must be something different from others' thinking.

- While preparing the above keep in mind the quality and caliber of participants of the meeting.

- Familiarize the points by repeatedly running through them in the mind.

- Define your objective very clearly. Valluvar has given a direction that your speech must achieve nothing short of 'bringing in' a change in the minds of the participants.

- Decide the flow. Where to start and how to end your speech.

- Incorporate the quotes of famous personalities relevant to the subject. This will make people to accept your point of view.

- If it is a PowerPoint Presentation make it with graphics to be attractive for the viewers.

- Anticipate the questions from the audience and be prepared with answers.

- One day earlier make a rehearsal of your speech. This is important.

- Arrive early at the meeting venue.

- Dress appropriately for the meeting. Your attire adds value to your points.

- Ensure your Laptop, pointer etc. functions well in the meeting hall.

This is what Valluvar means by his terminology 'ஆற்றின் அளவறிந்து கற்க' in this couplet.

Son: Thank you Dad for these wonderful points to help in preparing for a meeting. Valluvar also says 'அவையஞ்சா' meaning one should not fear in the meeting. But I always develop a fear complex when I go to the stage or rise in a meeting to talk. How to overcome this?

Father: Do not start the subject straight away. Greet the people on the dais. Tell about yourself briefly. Since these two are well known and familiar to you, you will settle down nicely to speak further. Start your subject with a confident note. I want to quote a saying here.

"While preparing for a speech you must assume that every participant is more knowledgeable than you; but, while delivering the speech you must feel that the participants have come here to hear your speech because you know better than them".

Now the fear will go.

Son: How to bring in a change in the minds of the participants? Is it not difficult?

Father: Yes son. It is difficult. This requires tangential thinking while preparing the speech. Look for all possible alternatives. Even a small value addition in the speech will make a difference. A deep study and analysis of the subject alone will help. Do not assume that whatever exists now is correct. Change is the only thing that remains constant and the change will come "from within" if you are at it.

Well prepared and fearless speech wins the audience!

Summing up the messages given above,

- A good communication must bind the audience.

- Powerful communicator is termed as learned among the learned.

- Competent communicator succeeds.

- Well-communicated jobs - well received by the subordinates

- Fearless delivery of a well-prepared speech brings in a change

Final Note:

It seems during Valluvar's period holding meetings was common, probably by the king or by the literary poets. Unless such events were prevalent in those days, a poet could not have given such inspiring advices on communication. Apparently, the governance of the Tamil kings in those days was so much advanced as to call for regular meetings!

Valluvar conveys how important the communication skill is!

VISION

10.0. Understanding Vision

Son: Dad, what is vision? Can you explain?

Father: No human being is born with a predetermined goal for life. As one grows, the ambitions and desires set a goal in one's life. Some of the ambitions settle very deeply into the mind, and as age grows it becomes a strong goal. This goal becomes a vision that drives an individual to work tirelessly, overcoming obstacles to achieve it. For some people, past experiences, especially failures ignite a fire within to achieve something against the failure. This becomes a vision for that individual.

On the other hand, setting a goal in business, working towards it and achieving the goal are also possible. For instance, an entrepreneur after starting a business may set a 'Sales Target' to be achieved in a particular period of time. This is called as 'Vision' of his company. Many organisations today adopt this kind of long-term vision approach. Generally, the goal should be ambitious, over and above what one can achieve in the normal course.

Valluvar provides guidance on setting the vision and the ways of achieving it. Let's look at the couplets.

10.1. Couplet: 540 / Chapter: 54
Unforgetfulness (பொச்சாவாமை)

உள்ளியது எய்தல் எளிதுமன் மற்றும்தான்
உள்ளியது உள்ளாப் பெறின்.

***The one who takes his goal deep into the mind
achieves it easily.***

Son: Dad, Valluvar says if the set goal is taken deep into one's own mind it is easy to achieve it. Am I right?

Father: Yes. You are right. As I already told you, the human mind is a very powerful weapon in the world. If someone determines to perform something from the bottom of his heart he can achieve it unmindful of its complexities and challenges. Valluvar says that if a thought or a target is taken into one's mind deeply he can achieve it easily. The same point has been emphasized by many writers like Joseph Murphy, Kopmeyer etc. Setting a long-term vision is crucial for business. No business can succeed without a clear goal. To achieve the vision, one must constantly focus on its objectives day and night and all through the year. Only then victory can be attained.

I can give a live example of this. One Mr.Chinni Krishnan from a town called Cuddalore in the state of Tamil Nadu in India, revolutionized the shampoo industry in 1978. He introduced shampoo in small sachets, making it affordable for the common man. He had a great vision for this product to reach the masses. He suddenly died in 1979. His wife and four young sons took on the challenge and pursued the vision of Mr. Chinni Krishnan. Despite financial struggles and competition from established brands like Godrej, out of their sheer hard work and dedication they successfully brought out the business. Today, the company, rebranded as "Kevin Care" in India has grown into a massive enterprise of Rs. 50,000 million Indian Rupee (about 600/- million USD) under the leadership of one of his sons Mr. C.K. Ranganathan. The sons carried their father's vision and made it a reality. This demonstrates Valluvar's words in this couplet.

Take deep in mind – Make things happen!

———•———

10.2 Couplet: 578 / Chapter: 58
The Vision (கண்ணோட்டம்)

கருமம் சிதையாமல் கண்ணோட வல்லார்க்கு
உரிமை உடைத்து இவ்வுலகு.

Anything can be achieved by the one who concentrates in his vision without any deviation.

Son: Same subject. Is it not?

Father: Not exactly. Many people deviate from the goals set by them and face failures in spite of dedicated work. Valluvar says only when the set target is pursued without any deviation it can be achieved. The individual must engage himself fully, with a clear vision and without an unwavering thought. Some people start a business with a goal in mind, but after some time they change the goal. Whatever efforts spent for the earlier target becomes a waste. Such people cannot achieve their goals because their actions get scattered. According to Valluvar, one's thoughts should always be focused on achieving a specific goal set by him.

Son: Is this point applicable to organisations also?

Father: Very much applicable. Today's management practices also emphasize the importance of having a clear vision. Organisations define their goals for the next three to five years and create a **"Vision Statement"** that outlines the objective of the company. This document is communicated not only to the management team but also to all the employees in the organisation to ensure that everyone is working towards the same goal. To maintain this focus, the organisations display the "Vision Statement" prominently in all vantage points in the company premises so that it does not miss the eyes of the employees. In some organisations, this is also made as a slogan to be chanted during the daily employee meetings. All these efforts will synergize the vision and will not allow it to deviate from the minds of everyone in the organisation. Once it is strongly taken into the minds of the employees they start working towards it. Many organisations have succeeded in achieving their goal only because all the employees marched towards the same goal without drifting.

This approach aligns with Valluvar's philosophy of highlighting the importance of a clear and unwavering vision in achieving success.

Frequent change of goal post - No goal was shot!

Summing up the messages given above,

- Set a VISION

- Take it deep into the mind

- Do not change the goal

Be a visionary and build a business empire!

Conclusion

Though Valluvar teaches discipline and virtuous life in his book Thirukkural, we can see that he mostly favours a materialistic life. He emphasizes the need for money in one's life and goes to the extent of saying "There is no place in this world for the one who has no money" through the following couplet.

அருளில்லார்க்கு அவ்வுலகம் இல்லை பொருளில்லார்க்கு இவ்வுலகம் இல்லாகி யாங்கு. (குறள் - 247)

The eternal world does not belong to GRACELESS people; similarly this world does not belong to MONEYLESS people.
(couplet - 247)

Money predominantly comes from business. To emphasize this point he has touched upon all the management aspects required to run a business like decision taking, effective performance, communication, training, skill development, performance appraisal etc. He has also touched upon Research and Development which is very unique for a poet like him.

On many occasions he is emphatic, sometimes he is suggestive, occasionally he is warning and mostly encouraging. His encouragement goes to the extent of challenging destiny, which, today's motivational speakers may hesitate to utter.

Having shared my fifty years of experience in management and also the success stories of global entrepreneurs, the book offers a practicality of ancient wisdom. Every couplet selected for this book distinctly differs from the other and every couplet preaches the intricacies of management.

This book was originally written in Tamil. Many of my friends and leading academicians encouraged me to write it in English to reach out to those who do not understand Tamil. Though, earlier I have written many technical articles and even written a technical book in English, translating the couplets of the great poet Thiruvalluvar, without changing its meaning was a tough task. Every couplet was touching the lives of human beings and translating such a sensitive subject conveying the intention of the author in its true spirit was a challenge to me. Still, I have made sincere efforts to ensure that the correct sense portrayed by Valluvar is conveyed.

This book will be of immense use to practicing managers, CEOs and more so to the 'Start-Ups'.

Chapters (அதிகாரங்கள்) used in this book

———◆———

Couplets Handled

1.1. **Couplet:** **467**	எண்ணித் துணிக கருமம் துணிந்தபின் எண்ணுவம் என்பது இழுக்கு. *Think before embarking on a job. It will be a blunder to think after embarking.*

1.2. **Couplet:** **675**	பொருள்கருவி காலம் வினைஇடனொடு ஐந்தும் இருள்தீர எண்ணிச் செயல் . *Before venturing, get absolute clarity on these five; the product, machinery, time, process and location.*

1.3. **Couplet:** **471**	வினைவலியும் தன்வலியும் மாற்றான் வலியும் துணைவலியும் தூக்கிச் செயல். *Accomplish a task by evaluating its toughness, own strength, opponent's strength and supporting strengths.*

1.4. **Couplet:** **462**	தெரிந்த இனத்தொடு தேர்ந்தெண்ணிச் செய்வார்க்கு அரும்பொருள் யாதொன்றும் இல். *No task is impossible to the one, who carefully selects the proper knowledge partner and performs.*

1.5. **Couplet:** **461**	அழிவதூஉம் ஆவதூஉம் ஆகி வழிபயக்கும் ஊதியமும் சூழ்ந்து செயல். *Consider the income, the expenses and the resulting profit before venturing into a business.*

1.6.
Couplet:
758

குன்றேறி யானைப்போர் கண்டற்றால் தன்கைத்தொன்று
உண்டாகச் செய்வான் வினை.

Doing business with own funds is as easy as watching an 'elephants fight' from the top of a hill.

1.7.
Couplet:
473

உடைத்தம் வலியறியார் ஊக்கத்தின் ஊக்கி
இடைக்கண் முரிந்தார் பலர்.

Many have failed in between for starting out of emotional impulse without evaluating own strength.

1.8.
Couplet:
760

ஒண்பொருள் காழ்ப்ப இயற்றியார்க்கு எண்பொருள்
ஏனை இரண்டும் ஒருங்கு.

For those who do honest business, besides money, virtuous life and eternal happiness will be bestowed.

1.9.
Couplet:
832

பேதைமையுள் எல்லாம் பேதைமை காதன்மை
கையல்ல தன்கண் செயல்.

It will be a folly among follies to involve in an act about which one is not passionate.

2.1.
Couplet:
547

இறைகாக்கும் வையகம் எல்லாம் அவனை
முறைகாக்கும் முட்டாச் செயின்.

A king will safeguard his country, but he will be safeguarded by the uninterrupted systems created by him.

2.2.
Couplet:
512

வாரி பெருக்கி வளம்படுத் துற்றவை
ஆராய்வான் செய்க வினை.

Let the one who brings in various sources of income, adds resources and handles the hurdles, manage.

2.3.
Couplet:
385

இயற்றலும் ஈட்டலும் காத்தலும் காத்த
வகுத்தலும் வல்லது அரசு.

A competent kingdom devises avenues of income,
collects, safeguards and apportions appropriately.

2.4.
Couplet:
520

நாடோறும் நாடுக மன்னன் வினைசெய்வான்
கோடாமை கோடாது உலகு.

A country will never go down if the king ensures motivation
of his functionaries as a matter of daily routine.

2.5.
Couplet:
1022

ஆள்வினையும் ஆன்ற அறிவும் எனஇரண்டின்
நீள்வினையான் நீளும் குடி.

Enhancement of both skill and insightful knowledge will
lead to enhanced livelihood of citizens.

2.6.
Couplet:
582

எல்லார்க்கும் எல்லாம் நிகழ்பவை எஞ்ஞான்றும்
வல்லறிதல் வேந்தன் தொழில்.

It is the duty of a king always to know thoroughly
aboutall the happenings happening around him.

2.7.
Couplet:
584

வினைசெய்வார் தம்சுற்றம் வேண்டாதார் என்றாங்கு
அனைவரையும் ஆராய்வது ஒற்று.

The job of a spy is not only to watch the enemies but also
to monitor the subordinates and relatives of the king.

2.8.
Couplet:
588

ஒற்றுஒற்றித் தந்த பொருளையும் மற்றுமோர்
ஒற்றினால் ஒற்றிக் கொளல்.

A king must verify and validate the information got by
one spy using another spy.

2.9.
Couplet:
445

சூழ்வார் கண் ணாக ஒழுகலான் மன்னவன்
சூழ்வாரைச் சூழ்ந்து கொளல்.

A king must be surrounded by good advisors since hesees the world through them.

2.10.
Couplet:
448

இடிப்பாரை இல்லாத ஏமரா மன்னன்
கெடுப்பார் இலானுங் கெடும்.

A king not having a critic around him doesn't require anyone else to spoil he will; will get spoiled on his own.

2.11.
Couplet:
447

இடிக்கும் துணையாரை ஆள்வாரை யாரே
கெடுக்கும் தகைமை யவர்?

"Who can spoil a king who knows how to handle the critics around him?

2.12.
Couplet:
889

எட்பக வன்ன சிறுமைத்தே ஆயினும்
உட்பகை உள்ளதாங் கேடு.

However tiny the internal enmity be it is dangerous.

2.13.
Couplet:
653

ஒஓதல் வேண்டும் ஒளிமாழ்கும் செய்வினை
ஆஅது என்னு மவர்.

One who aspires a great position in life will not indulge in acts that will spoil his credibility.

3.1.
Couplet:
631

கருவியும் காலமும் செய்கையும் செய்யும்
அருவினையும் மாண்டது அமைச்சு.

A good ministry outperforms even impossible tasks by deploying right tool, right method, at the right time.

3.2.
Couplet:
687

கடனறிந்து காலம் கருதி இடனறிந்து
எண்ணி உரைப்பான் தலை.

A good leader assigns after understanding the job time factor and evaluating the location.

3.3.
Couplet:
770

நிலைமக்கள் சால உடைத்தெனினும் தானை
தலைமக்கள் இல்வழி இல்.

Even though the army has longstanding soldiers if there is no leader no way forward.

3.4.
Couplet:
634

தெரிதலும் தேர்ந்து செயலும் ஒருதலையாச்
சொல்லலும் வல்லது அமைச்சு.

A competent manager is the one who understands (the job), chooses the right method and communicates head on.

3.5.
Couplet:
468

ஆற்றின் வருந்தா வருத்தம் பலர்நின்று
போற்றினும் பொத்துப் படும்.

A project started without a strategy will fail even if more hands are deployed.

3.6.
Couplet:
637

செயற்கை அறிந்தக் கடைத்தும் உலகத்து
இயற்கை அறிந்து செயல்.

Even though one knows all the rules and regulations, he must be practical while performing.

3.7.
Couplet:
691

அகலாது அணுகாது தீக்காய்வார் போல்க
இகல்வேந்தர்ச் சேர்ந்தொழுகு வார்.

Move with the king like one who neither goes closer nor moves away from fire while warming.

**4.1.
Couplet:
633**

பிரித்தலும் பேணிக் கொளலும் பிரிந்தார்ப்
பொருத்தலும் வல்லது அமைச்சு.

*A good management is one which takes out,
takes care, takes back and fits well.*

**4.2.
Couplet:
517**

இதனை இதனால் இவன்முடிக்கும் என்றாய்ந்து
அதனை அவன்கண் விடல்.

*Let the job be assigned to one after evaluating that he
will complete this job because of these reasons.*

**4.3.
Couplet:
515**

அறிந்தாற்றிச் செய்கிற்பாற்கு அல்லால் வினைதான்
சிறந்தானென்று ஏவற்பாற் றன்று.

*Don't depute the one who doesn't know the ways and means
of performing a job, Just because he is aware of the job.*

**4.4.
Couplet:
528**

பொதுநோக்கான் வேந்தன் வரிசையா நோக்கின்
அதுநோக்கி வாழ்வார் பலர்.

*A king, instead of treating everyone at par, treats
serially on merits, many will strive to be meritorious.*

**4.5.
Couplet:
518**

வினைக்குரிமை நாடிய பின்றை அவனை
அதற்குரிய னாகச் செயல்.

*When a person is assigned a position, make him
responsible for that position.*

**4.6.
Couplet:
698**

இளையர் இனமுறையர் என்றிகழார் நின்ற
ஒளியோடு ஒழுகப் படும்.

*One should be respected for his position rather
than scorning him for being young or belonging to a
particular race.*

4.7.
Couplet:
514

எனைவகையான் தேறியக்கண்ணும்
வினைவகையான் வேறாகும் மாந்தர் பலர்.

Irrespective of the tough selection process, everyone got selected will execute the same job differently.

4.8.
Couplet:
562

கடிதோச்சி மெல்ல எறிக நெடிதாக்கம்
நீங்காமை வேண்டு பவர்.

Pretend big and punish less, if the benefit of one's long service is not to be parted with.

4.9.
Couplet:
550

கொலையிற் கொடியாரை வேந்தொறுத்தல் பைங்கூழ்
களைகட் டதனொடு நேர்.

A king eliminating the terrorists is as good as a farmer removing the weeds to safeguard the crops.

5.1.
Couplet:
465

வகையறச் சூழாது எழுதல் பகைவரைப்
பாத்திப் படுப்பதோர் ஆறு.

Waging a war without a strategy will channelize the entry of the enemy.

5.2.
Couplet:
750

எனைமாட்சித் தாகியக் கண்ணும் வினைமாட்சி
இல்லார்கண் இல்லது அரண்.

Irrespective of having special protections, if an effective war strategy is lacking, the bulwark will fail.

5.3.
Couplet:
684

அறிவுரு ஆராய்ந்த கல்வி இம்மூன்றன்
செறிவுடையான் செல்க வினைக்கு .

The one having good general knowledge, good personality and in-depth subject knowledge must go as an ambassador.

5.4.

Couplet: 769

சிறுமையும் செல்லாத் துனியும் வறுமையும்
இல்லாயின் வெல்லும் படை.

*An army will win if it does not have soldiers lesser in
numbers, hating their own king and poverty-stricken.*

5.5.

Couplet: 682

அன்பறிவு ஆராய்ந்த சொல்வன்மை
தூதுரைப்பார்க்கு
இன்றி யமையாத மூன்று.

*The inevitable qualities of an emissary will be
kindness, knowledge and competent communication.*

5.6.

Couplet: 685

தொகச்சொல்லித் தூவாத நீக்கி நகச்சொல்லி
நன்றி பயப்பதாம் தூது.

*A good emissary collates, explains, eliminates irrelevancies
and communicates cheerfully to derive the benefit.*

5.7.

Couplet: 689

விடுமாற்றம் வேந்தர்க்கு உரைப்பான் வடுமாற்றம்
வாய்சோரா வன்க ணவன்.

*The right emissary never utters a faulty word even by
mistake while communicating with the other king.*

6.1.

Couplet: 678

வினையான் வினையாக்கிக் கோடல் நனைகவுள்
யானையால் யானையாத் தற்று.

*Completing a job along with another job, is like capturing
an elephant using another elephant.*

6.2.

Couplet: 663

கடைக்கொட்கச் செய்தக்கது ஆண்மை இடைக்கொட்கின்
ஏற்றா விழுமம் தரும்.

*A good management reveals (its' developments) at the end;
revealing in-between yields negative results.*

6.3.
Couplet:
611

அருமை உடைத்தென்று அசாவாமை வேண்டும்
பெருமை முயற்சி தரும்.

Never give up a task because it is tough;
efforts bring glory.

6.4.
Couplet:
676

முடிவும் இடையூறும் முற்றியாங் கெய்தும்
படுபயனும் பார்த்துச் செயல்.

Perform by considering the target, hurdles and the benefits
derived on accomplishment.

6.5.
Couplet:
662

ஊறொரால் உற்றபின் ஒல்காமை இவ்விரண்டின்
ஆறென்பர் ஆய்ந்தவர் கோள்.

The trait of a researcher is to take precautions against
anticipated failures and not to worry if fails.

7.1.
Couplet:
677

செய்வினை செய்வான் செயல்முறை அவ்வினை
உள்ளறிவான் உள்ளம் கொளல்.

One who wants to perform effectively learns from the one
who has deep knowledge on the subject.

7.2.
Couplet:
672

தூங்குக தூங்கிச் செயற்பால தூங்கற்க
தூங்காது செய்யும் வினை.

Delay the jobs which can be delayed; don't delay
the jobs which should not be delayed.

7.3.
Couplet:
668

கலங்காது கண்ட வினைக்கண் துளங்காது
தூக்கம் கடிந்து செயல்.

Once decided without ambiguity, complete the job without
further delay"

7.4.
Couplet:
670

எனைத்திட்பம் எய்தியக் கண்ணும் வினைத்திட்பம்
வேண்டாரை வேண்டாது உலகு.

*Despite having all competencies, if unable to complete
a job effectively, he gets rejected.*

7.5.
Couplet:
640

முறைப்படச் சூழ்ந்தும் முடிவிலவே செய்வர்
திறப்பாடு இலாஅ தவர்.

*Incompetency leads to incomplete jobs despite
adhering to all procedures.*

7.6.
Couplet:
483

அருவினை என்ப உளவோ கருவியான்
காலம் அறிந்து செயின்?

*Is there any impossible task, if the right tool is deployed
at the right time?*

7.7.
Couplet:
490

கொக்கொக்க கூம்பும் பருவத்து மற்றதன்
குத்தொக்க சீர்த்த விடத்து.

*Like a crane awaiting the right prey, one must
await the ripe juncture to act.*

7.8.
Couplet:
673

ஒல்லும்வாய் எல்லாம் வினை நன்றே ஒல்லாக்கால்
செல்லும்வாய் நோக்கிச் செயல்.

*Whenever possible carry on the job; If not, at least
make progress towards the goal.*

7.9.
Couplet:
489

எய்தற்கு அரியது இயைந்தக்கால் அந்நிலையே
செய்தற்கு அரிய செயல்.

*If the right opportunity comes up that is the right time
to complete even a rare job.*

8.1.
Couplet:
619

தெய்வத்தான் ஆகாது எனினும் முயற்சிதன்
மெய்வருத்தக் கூலி தரும்.

*Even if God declines, one's efforts with hard work
will yield results.*

8.2.
Couplet:
772

கான முயலெய்த அம்பினில் யானை
பிழைத்த வேல் ஏந்தல் இனிது.

*Better to carry a spear which misses an elephant
rather than an arrow which kills a rabbit.*

8.3.
Couplet:
612

வினைக்கண் வினைகெடல் ஓம்பல் வினைக்குறை
தீர்ந்தாரின் தீர்ந்தன்று உலகு.

*After eying a job to be tough, anyone quitting
will be discarded by the society.*

8.4.
Couplet:
666

எண்ணிய எண்ணியாங்கு எய்துப எண்ணியார்
திண்ணியர் ஆகப் பெறின்.

*The one with mental determination performs
exactly as planned.*

8.5
Couplet:
593

ஆக்கம் இழந்தேமென்று அல்லாவார் ஊக்கம்
ஒருவந்தம் கைத்துடை யார்.

*The one who has motivation built within him will not
get dejected even when facing failures.*

8.6.
Couplet:
661

வினைத்திட்பம் என்ப தொருவன் மனத்திட்பம்
மற்றைய எல்லாம் பிற.

*Effective performance is a mental factor
others no matter.*

8.7.
Couplet:
620

ஊழையும் உப்பக்கம் காண்பர் உலைவின்றித்
தாழாது உளுற்று பவர்.

*He who puts his efforts relentlessly without fear
will chase and see off the destiny.*

9.1.
Couplet:
722

கற்றாருள் கற்றார் எனப்படுவர் கற்றார்முன்
கற்ற செலச் சொல்லு வார்.

Those who could drive home a point to a learned gathering will be termed as learned among the learned.

9.2.
Couplet:
647

சொலல் வல்லன் சோர்விலன் அஞ்சானவனை
இகல்வெல்லல் யார்க்கும் அரிது.

It is impossible to win the one who is a good communicator, not lazy and fearless.

9.3.
Couplet:
648

விரைந்து தொழில்கேட்கும் ஞாலம் நிரந்தினிது
சொல்லுதல் வல்லார்ப் பெறின்.

Everyone will be eager to receive a task from the one who explains well with a smiling face.

9.4.
Couplet:
725

ஆற்றின் அளவறிந்து கற்க அவையஞ்சா
மாற்றம் கொடுத்தற் பொருட்டு.

Prepare for a meeting understanding depth of the subject, convey courageously, in such a way to bring in a change.

10.1.
Couplet:
540

உள்ளியது எய்தல் எளிதுமன் மற்றும்தான்
உள்ளியது உள்ளப் பெறின்.

The one who takes his goal deep into the mind achieves it easily.

10.2.
Couplet:
578

கருமம் சிதையாமல் கண்ணோட வல்லார்க்கு
உரிமை உடைத்து இவ்வுலகு.

Anything can be achieved by the one who concentrates in his vision without any deviation.

Additional Couplets Used

1.0
Couplet:
1031

சுழன்றும் ஏர்ப்பின்னது உலகம் அதனால்
உழந்தும் உழவே தலை.

*Though the earth is spinning, it is behind a plough only;
therefore agriculture leads the world.*

1.6
Couplet :
423

எப்பொருள் யார்யார்வாய்க் கேட்பினும் அப்பொருள்
மெய்ப்பொருள் காண்பது அறிவு.

*Irrespective of whoever has said a subject, it is wise to
understand the truthful meaning of that subject.*

1.8
Couplet :
292

பொய்மையும் வாய்மை யிடத்த புரைதீர்ந்த
நன்மை பயக்கும் எனின்.

*Even a lie will take the place of truth,
if it brings blameless benefit.*

5.7
Couplet:
100

இனிய உளவாக இன்னாத கூறல்
கனியிருப்பக் காய்கவர்ந் தற்று.

*Using bad words when good words are available is like
eating raw vegetables when ripe fruits are available*

9.0
Couplet:
643

கேட்டார் பிணிக்கும் தகைவாய்க் கேளாரும்
வேட்ப மொழிவதாம் சொல்.

*An oration must bind the audience to the speaker and
make those who missed it long for hearing it.*

Conclude
Couplet:
247

அருளில்லார்க்கு அவ்வுலகம் இல்லை
பொருளில்லார்க்கு இவ்வுலகம் இல்லாகி யாங்கு.

*The eternal world does not belong to GRACELESS people;
similarly this world does not belong to MONEYLESS people.*

———•••———

Management Concepts Explained

www.ingramcontent.com/pod-product-compliance
Lightning Source LLC
Chambersburg PA
CBHW031119130726
47988CB00006B/2145

9798896999201